ABOARD MEGA-9, THREE PEOPLE WERE CELEBRATING A FAMOUS ESCAPE...

A TOAST, MY FRIENDS... *TO US*! IT'S FIVE YEARS AGO, ALMOST TO THE MINUTE, THAT WE ESCAPED FROM THE MEKON'S PYRAMID!

D1485952

DAN DARE, DESCENDANT OF THE LEGENDARY SPACE HERO, WAS WITH HIS FRIENDS SUGAR JOE ROBINSON AND LIEUTENANT HELEN SCOTT.

AT ONE TIME, I THOUGHT NONE OF US WOULD GET AWAY...

WITH *DAN DARE* LEADING US, I WAS NEVER WORRIED...*MUCH*!

YOU SAY THE NICEST THINGS!

ON THAT OCCASION, WE SURE SORTED OUT A FEW TREENS. ONE DAY, WE'LL MAKE CERTAIN WE DEAL WITH THEM *PERMANENTLY*!

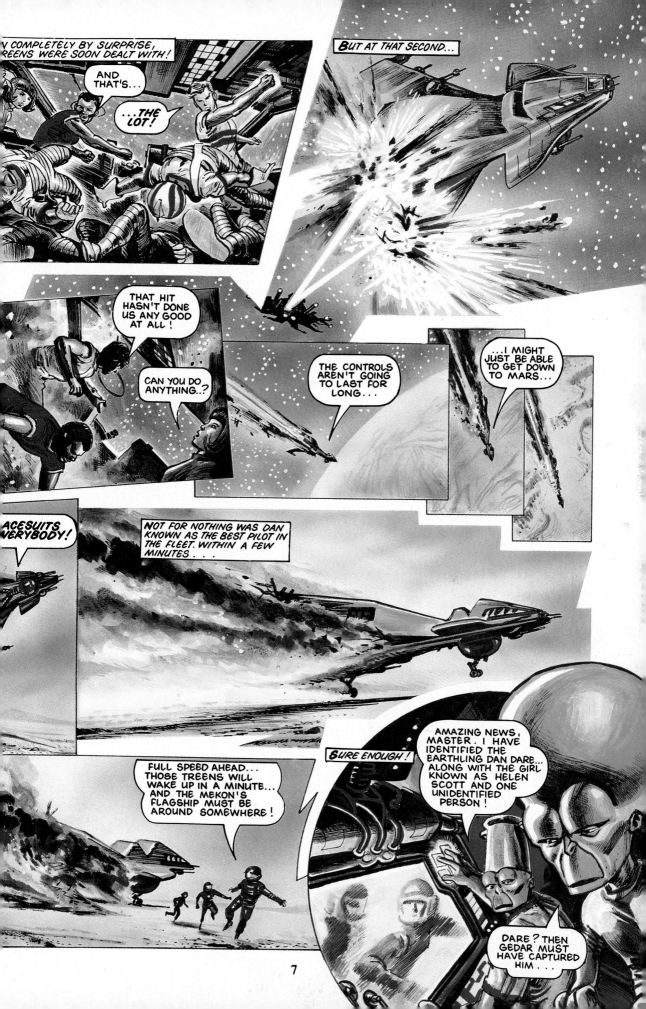

8

BACK IN HIS FLAT, SUMMERFIELD DECIDED TO RID HIMSELF OF THE MENACE. BUT...

"ITS SIGHTLESS EYES ARE HEARTLESS KILLERS, UNLESS THE VICTIM IS BLESSED OF MIRRORS."

THE SKULL'S TRYING TO KILL ME!

I'LL THROW IT IN THE RIVER. NO— IT'S ALIVE... MY EYES— FEEL DIZZY!

SUDDENLY, HE FOUND ONE OF HIS COLLECTION OF DAGGERS CLOSE TO HIS THROAT—

THE- THE CURSE IS FORCING ME TO STAB MYSELF!

"...UNLESS THE VICTIM IS -IS BL[ESSED] OF MIRRORS". ONE CHANCE IF I JUST TURN T[HE] BLADE...

THEN HE REMEMBERED THE WORDS OF THE CURSE...

THE LIGHT WAS SUDDENLY REFLECTED OFF THE BLADE AND BACK INTO THE SKULL LIKE A BOLT OF LIGHTNING...

THE HIDEOUS THING IS SCREAMING... I'VE KILLED IT!

NWAAARRGHHH!

IT'S ALL DONE WITH MIRRORS, THEY SAY, SUMMERFIELD CERTA[INLY] PROVED IT. BY THE WA[Y] HE SOLD POOR MAK[E] BURNT OUT SKULL TO [HIM] FOR £1. FOR SOM[E] REASON HE'D TAK[EN] A DISLIKE TO IT[.]

The End

12

DALEY DOZEN

12

A lot can happen between now and the Olympics in Los Angeles in 1984. But barring illness and accidents, here are 12 athletes who should come back home with medals glinting on their chests.

One man who gets any vote is Sebastian Coe, the world's No.1 middle distance runner, a marvel of specialised physical efficiency. He intends to move up to 5,000m in the Los Angeles Olympics.

High on the list is Britain's No.1 girl sprinter, Kathy Smallwood, who won gold medals in competitions in China and Japan and an Olympic bronze at Moscow. She was 1980's woman athlete of the year.

DALEY DOZEN 12

A world record breaker over 1,500m and two miles is Steve Ovett. He won the 800m at Moscow. He'll get more medals in L.A.

An athlete whom everyone is expecting great things of at Los Angeles is Steve Cram. He, Keith Connor and Daley were Britain's gold medallists at the European Championsh in 1982. If he keeps up his form, this boy will be among the winners in the USA.

Cameron Sharp became Scotland's 200 metres silver medallist at the European Championships in Athens in 1982. Experts have predicted a devastating future for him, and Daley's with them.

dy
ermore and
ght) Linsey
cdonald

David
Moorcroft

HEINZ
6

NIKE

CITIZEN
2

12 A DALEY DOZEN

y Livermore and Linsey Macdonald are
girls with a lot going for them. Judy
ame the British and Commonwealth
tathlon record holder in 1982. Linsey
be only 20 when the Los Angeles
mpics arrive. At Moscow she reached
finals and won a bronze in the relay.
's hoping her Moscow bronze will turn
he glint of gold.

When Dave Moorcroft became the world record
holder of the 5,000m in 13 minutes 0.42 seconds,
everybody knew this runner was going places. He
told Daley then that he was hoping to do just as
well — if not better — in the years to come.
Running and competing are things he does well,
and Daley thinks he'll be okay at Los Angeles. At
his peak, in fact!

15

Keith Connor is another British athlete who took the European and Commonwealth gold medals in his triple jump event. Those were Britain's first gold medals in the event since T.J. Ahearne won the Olympic title in 1908. And that Commonwealth Games leap was the second longest ever, although most reckon Keith's got the ability, dedication and drive to go one better!

Before 1982 Tessa Sanderson must have thought that her athletics' world was very rosy. Not only was she the British and Commonwealth Women's Javelin Champion, with a throw of 69.70 metres, she had also set a UK best in the Heptathlon, the 7 event elongated pentathlon for women. But a catalogue of misfortune during 1982 included becoming jobless when she lost her coaching job because of her sports' club's closure, and being ruled out of both the European Championships and Commonwealth Games through injury to her achilles tendon and then a broken bone in her left elbow. Tessa has since bounced back and a good performance in Los Angeles, if selected, would more than make up for all her bad luck.

And athlete No.13 is Daley Thompson himself, World decathlon champion in 1982. By his own admission, there's still room for improvement in the decathlon, so maybe he'll break the world points' record again. It'll be great if he gets the chance to do it at the games in L.A. in 1984.

Britain's hurdles queen is Shirley Strong (above). She won a gold medal at the 1982 Commonwealth Games in Brisbane and her time of 12.78 seconds was a Games' record. She ought to be at Los Angeles, as should Allan Wells (right), the gold medal-winning sprinter who has been going from victory to victory. His Moscow gold in 1980 for the 100 metres could be repeated at the next Games.

A DALEY DOZEN

12

You can follow the Olympics and all the other great sporting events in your EAGLE comic every week!

FALLING FOR THE FALL GUY . . .

Colt Seavers, stuntman, bounty hunter and crime fighter, goes through some pretty hairy moments to keep us all happy in The Fall Guy TV series. But although Colt is played by former Bionic Man, Lee Majors, it isn't Lee who performs the risky stunts. Those are left to a couple of professional stuntmen, Mickey Gilbert and Bob Bralver.

These two have pulled quite a stunt in the actual making of the series, as it's the stories that have to fit Mickey and Bob's ideas for stunts and not, as you might expect, the other way around. They've come up with some really tricky ideas, too, like jumping Colt's car on to a moving railway wagon to allow him to escape from a town where the baddies had blocked off the roads.

That called for a computer to work out the speeds of the car and train, and to give the exact angle needed for the ramp to launch the car into the air.

Despite all the danger, the only serious injury to any of Bob and Mickey's 30-odd back-up team of stuntmen has been a broken arm. Let's hope Bob and Mickey never break up so we can carry on being thrilled by their daring work!

WHO'S THIS, THEN?

No doubt they would really heckle you if you can't come up with their names, so can you spot who this pair are in the double negative pic? (Solution below).

Unscramble the words in the box on the right and find out which one is not a dog.

NIASLAAT
FIFATSM
XERBO
HDUEYRGNO
YKONDE

EAGLE BOOK OF RECORDS

Dear EAGLE,

I have enclosed a copy of the magazine which I drew, printed and sold. I am only 11, and I wondered if I was the youngest writer to sell something? **Dan, Bristol.**

It's a great mag, Dan, but the youngest commercially published writer according to the 'Guinness Book of Records', was Dorothy Straight from Washington D.C. who wrote a book called 'How The World Began', published in 1964. She was just 4 years old at the time!

WRITING ON THE WALL DE...

Judging by the walls and advertising hoardings dotted around the country, it's clear that graffiti rules, okay! And here's a selection of okay graffiti sent in by Bruce of Cleveland.

AMNESIA RULES, O . . .
ER . . . UM . . .
JAMES BOND RULES, O.O.K.
APATHY RU . . .
SALIVA DROOLS, O.K.
FRENCH DOCKERS RULE, AU QUAI.
THE TOWN CRYER RULES, OKEZ, OKEZ, OKEZ.

Thanks, Bruce, and you've won yourself £3, which we're sure is okay with you!

IT'LL BE ALL RIGHT IN THE ISSUE . . .

Most of our photo-stories work out really well, but every once in a while, things go just a little wrong. We've selected a few of those moments for you . . .

♪ . . . YOU PUT YOUR LEFT LEG IN . . . ♪

I MUST BE LOSING WEIGHT — MY ENERGISER RING'S JUST DROPPED OFF!

OOOPS! I WAS SUPPOSED TO KICK IT IN THE OTHER TEAM'S GOAL!

IAN'S FILM QUIZ

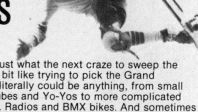

CRAZY CRAZES

Trying to forecast just what the next craze to sweep the country will be is a bit like trying to pick the Grand National winner. It literally could be anything, from small items like Rubik Cubes and Yo-Yos to more complicated equipment like C.B. Radios and BMX bikes. And sometimes shopkeepers have stocked up with items they think are sure-fire winners only to find that, for some reason, they just don't catch on.

This happened to something called Pomma Wonga, a device that was going to swept the nation but ended up being swept into a lot of shopkeeper's dustbins!

One of the longer lasting fads has been the skateboard. It's still with us, with regular competitions still held and, as the picture shows, it provides spectacular action when an expert is on board. Just what the craze of '85 will be is anyone's guess, but if you can skateboard and at the same time solve a Rubik Cube, make contact on a C.B. and keep a Yo-Yo on the go, you'll probably be one of the first to find out!

. Which TV superhero plays he part of Hercules in the ew film of the same name?
) Spiderman.
) The Hulk.
) Dangermouse.

. Who was the director who rought E.T. and Eliott ogether in last year's big lm, E.T. — The Extra-errestrial?
Mel Brooks.
George Lucas.
Steven Spielberg.

Peter Sellers returned to e screen in The Trail of the nk Panther, but what is the me of his martial arts acher forever surprising e detective with his acks?
Cato.
Plato.
Nato.

Superman III is now with , but think back to Super-n II for a moment. What likely event happened to Superhero?
He was defeated.
He turned villain.
He got married.

Remember Tron? Which of following was a game yed in the Video World?
The light cycle game.
Video scrabble.
Computer Kim's game.

6. Star Wars III is coming around but we've seen the actor who played Ben Kenobi on TV as a spy. Which spy?
a) James Bond.
b) George Smiley.
c) The man from U.N.C.L.E.

7. Which member of the Star Trek team makes a dramatic recovery in the third Star Trek film?
a) Scottie.
b) Mr Spock.
c) Captain Kirk.

8. And finally, here's an oldie. The pic below is from a very famous western, but which one?
a) Blazing Saddles.
b) The Good, The Bad And The Ugly.
c) Butch Cassidy And The Sundance Kid.

The puzzle below consists of two squares joined together, and one of them has been divided diagonally. Study the shaded area and see if you can divide it into 4 equal sections.

I THOUGHT THE SCRIPT SAID BATTLEFIELD, NOT CATTLEFIELD!

ANSWERS TO PUZZLES

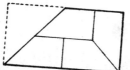

WHO'S THIS, THEN? — Muppet stars Stadtler and Waldorff DOG PUZZLE — DONKEY! The others are: ALSATIAN; BOXER; GREY-HOUND and MASTIFF. FILM QUIZ — 1,b. 2,c. 3, a. 4, c. 5, a. 6, b. 7, b. 8, c. SQUARES PUZZLES — If the shaded area is divided as shown in our diagram, you will see that each section consists of one square and one trian-gle. See diagram on right.

THE INVISIBLE BOY

THE driver dropped down a gear and accelerated into the bend at seventy-five miles an hour. The car heeled over, tyres screaming for a grip on the damp, leaf-strewn tarmac. Lying curled up in the boot, Tim Talbot braced himself against the wheel-arch and tried to ease his body away from the toolbag that was squashed hard up against his spine. It was hot in the boot, and decidedly cramped too, even for a boy of Tim's slim proportions. His right forefinger ached as well, from the strain of keeping the lid slightly open so that enough air could get in for him to be able to breathe properly.

The fact that Tim was lying *invisible* in the back of the car made absolutely no difference to how queasy and frightened he was feeling.

"There's no doubt," he thought as the driver pitched his vehicle into another bend at maniac speed, "that my power of invisibility can be distinctly dangerous at times. Sometimes I wish it had never happened."

Tim's Dad was an electrical research engineer, and one day while messing about in the laboratory, Tim had switched on some ultra-sensitive machinery and been subjected to the full blast of a Photon-Force Bombarder. Result? Complete invisibility for Tim every time his skin came into contact with a specially-developed micro-cell battery which he carried with him at all times. It was a strange, uncanny power, and one that Tim had always kept a close secret.

Once again, the car lurched under a violent change of direction, and Tim blinked invisibly as his head banged against a metal strut. "These two crooks," he thought miserably, "must be making one of the fastest getaways in the history of crime. Why the *heck* did I have to get involved?"

It had all started earlier that evening in Tim's house. He'd been settling down to watch the telly when Professor Watkins arrived. Watkins was a scientist friend of his dad, a bald, gnome-like figure whose conversation consisted of engineering formulae and nothing else. Soon the two men were lost in a scientific world of their own, talking — as far as Tim was con-cerned — a load of educated mumbo-jumbo. The telly, of course, had been switched off and stayed switched off.

After a boring hour or so, Tim got to his feet. "Dad," he said loudly, "can I go down to the chippy?"

"The what?"

"The fish and chip shop. I'm hungry."

Mr Talbot waved an impatient hand. "Don't be ridiculous, Tim, you only had your tea an hour ago. Greasy food is bad for you at this time of night."

"Exactly," said Professor Watkins with a knowing nod of his head. "Bad for the digestion — it's a proven scientific fact."

"Rhubarb," thought Tim rudely, but it was a thought that did him no something else, and his jaw went slack with surprise and shock.

At the far end of the laboratory, which was still in darkness, a man was climbing swiftly out of an open window. He was young, agile, his face white and tense. Under one arm he clutched a large, bulky file of papers bound with white tape. Even as Tim watched, the man vaulted a shrub less than five metres away and made a sprint for the street. He didn't even see young Tim, so intent he was on getting away. But by passing so close, he'd given the youngster a good close-up view of the bulky file which was still tucked under his arm.

It took a brief split-second to read what was on the cover. 'TOP-SECRET', it said boldly across the top. And underneath, in slightly smaller letters . . . 'TALBOT ENERGISING PROCESS — DATA AND FORMULAE'.

"Cripes," thought Tim, swallowing hard, "that's Dad's new cheap industrial heating scheme."

The man clutched a large, bulky file as he sprinted for the street.

"Rhubarb to that, too," thought Tim even more rudely. "I'm not making coffee and sandwiches for that old gnome. He's probably as absent-minded as Dad is, which means that as soon as the pair of them start yattering about the new energising whatsit, they'll forget they even asked me for a snack. And even if they do, I'll still have plenty of time to nip down to the chippy for a quick nosh-up!"

Grinning to himself, Tim shrugged into an anorak and headed for the back door. As he did all his research work from home, Mr Talbot's laboratory had been built on as an extension to his house. Just as Tim was heading for the front gate, he saw the lights go on in the lab as his father and Professor Watkins walked into the tiny reception area. Then Tim saw

ood at all, for his father added uickly: "The Professor and I have lot to talk about — my new nergising process for the cheap nd effective heating of industrial lants. Make us some coffee and andwiches in a few minutes, will ou? We'll be in the lab!" And with curt nod at his son, Talbot teered his guest quickly out of the oom.

PHANTOM PASSENGER

WITHOUT stopping to think, the youngster gave chase. He didn't know precisely what was going on, but one thing was sure. The man — whoever he was — had broken into Mr Talbot's laboratory, cracked the combination lock of the wall-safe and stolen that file. "No time to get help right now," thought Tim grimly, "I must try and keep that perisher in sight."

The thief was already in the street, running fast towards a junction fifty metres away. There, parked without lights in the shadow of a high hedge, was a fast, brand-new saloon car. Tim saw the car as he emerged from the glow of a street-lamp. The thief had reached the passenger door and was yanking it open. Tim came to a decision in a flash. Somehow he had to get into that car. And the only way to do it was to use his amazing power. *To make himself invisible!*

The all-important micro-cell battery was wrapped carefully in a handkerchief. Tim swiftly unfolded the cloth and wrapped the fingers of his right hand tightly round the tiny cell. The chemical reaction was immediate and intense. Flashes of inner power seemed to flow and explode through every molecule of Tim's body. There was a violent, throbbing surge of energy and then . . . it happened! Quite suddenly, the street looked empty. The Invisible Boy had come into his own!

Flashes of inner power seemed to flow through Tim's body as he clenched the micro-cell. . .

Like a flitting phantom, Tir closed swiftly on the rear of th parked car. The thief was sitting i the passenger seat, panting, get ting his breath back. The drive was switching on the ignition ready for a fast take-off. Even a Tim pressed the button of the boc lid and raised it slightly, he coul hear the driver's eager, excite question: "How did it go, Phil? Di you get it?"

"Yeah, it's right here." The thie tapped the bulky file with obviou pleasure. "No bother at all. I ha the safe open in seven minutes fla grabbed the papers and took o like a hare. The Gruber Corpora tion will pay a fortune for old Ta bot's new heating scheme."

As he squeezed himself into th cramped space of the car boot an lowered the lid to within a fev inches of its closing position, Tir realised what he had come u against. The two men were *indus trial spies!* Professional thieves i the pay of a ruthless busines organisation who were determine to steal Mr Talbot's new proces and introduce it as their own inver tion before it had been legally pat ented.

TRAPPED

"**B**ETTER get a move or Laurie," the thief said fror the passenger seat. "I wa almost rumbled back there b Talbot and a mate of his. They know by now that the file is mis ing."

"Okay." The driver revved th engine brutally, slammed it int gear and hit the accelerator peda with all the force he could muste "We'll get out of the area real fas Take the main drag to Buxton the head west . . . *flat out!*"

And flat out it had been — as Tir Talbot now had the bruises t prove. Once again he shifted hi position in the boot and tried t move the toolbag away from th sharp curve of his spine. His finge ached monotonously now, fror the constant strain of keeping th boot lid open just far enough fc the air to circulate inside.

"We must have gone thirt miles," thought Tim bleakly. "W must be stopping soon, surely. When the car *did* stop, he had n clear idea of what he'd do nex "Stay invisible, I suppose," h mused thoughtfully. "Try and fin out the address of the crook hideout and then contact the . . YAAAOW!"

Tim couldn't help his sudde wince of pain. As the car hit bump, the sharp-edged boot li swung down on its hinges and du hard into his sorely-tried forefir ger. Involuntarily, Tim pulled hi

22

The heavy toolbag hurtled through the air at the crooks as if thrown by a ghost.

Phil and Laurie ran down the street after the floating file.

finger close and rubbed it hard to restore the circulation. It was just then that the car hit *another* bump. Again, the boot lid swung down on its hinges, and this time . . . it clicked shut, trapping Tim helplessly inside.

The boy cursed silently under his breath. He was in trouble now, and he knew it only too well. Soon — very soon — the air inside the boot would be exhausted. He would become sleepy, lose consciousness, and then . . . well that would be it. Tim knew there was only one thing he could do. He would have to attract the thieves' attention and make them stop the car. But there was a problem. In his invisible state, Tim automatically lost all power of speech. He couldn't laugh, talk, croak or even grunt. He'd tried it before many times, but always in vain. While unseen, he was *unheard*, too!

THE CHASE!

WRIGGLING sideways, Tim began to beat his clenched fist rhythmically on the fibre board which protected the reverse side of the car's rear seats. A dull thudding noise echoed through the interior of the car.

"Do you hear what I hear?" said the driver with a scowl.

"Yeah, it seems to be coming from the boot. Pull over and let's have a look."

The car happened to be passing through a small town, and it shud-dered swiftly to a halt near the entrance to a large shopping precinct. It was nearly nine o'clock, dark, damp and with very few people on the streets.

The two thieves walked straight to the rear of the car, pushed the button and jerked the boot lid up.

"Nothing there," said Phil angrily. "Just the toolbag, like always."

"Maybe a few of the spanners were rattling," said Laurie."

"You're both wrong," thought Invisible Tim grimly. "Now cop this! It's been giving me backache for the past hour!" Lifting the heavy toolbag with both hands, he chucked it straight up and out at the stooping crooks. To Phil and Laurie, it seemed as if a poltergeist was at work. Spanners came hurtling out of the open neck of the bag and sliced the air at their heads. A couple of screwdrivers bounced off Phil's shoulder and landed with a clang in the gutter.

Both men reeled back, speechless and shaken. Tim was already climbing out of the boot, cursing the stiffness in his invisible limbs. "Got to reach the passenger seat before they get their wits back," he thought. "I can grab Dad's file and be off like a shot."

And that's just what he did. Phil and Laurie stood there like tailors' dummies as the bulky file of papers seemed to lift itself effortlessly out through the open car window and float swiftly away in mid-air along the street. Tim had covered a hundred metres before the villains made a move. Then they broke into a wild, disbelieving gallop. "It ain't natural," yelled Phil as he ran. "What's making that file float? A current of *air*?"

"Dunno," muttered Laurie, "but whatever it is I aim to find out. An' I aim to get them papers back, they're worth a *fortune* to us!"

Up ahead, Tim heard the pounding of their feet and increased his speed. Gaining a few more metres, he whisked round a corner and gave an inward whoop of delight. Across the street a bright, neon sign shone steadily above an arched brick doorway. The sign said simply: 'POLICE'. The hand of fate, it seemed, had guided the Invisible Boy to the local cop shop!

FLOATING FILE

TIM dashed towards the station entrance, a plan of action already formulating in his mind. A plan that would see the file of papers safely back in his father's safe *and* bring the thieves to justice at the same time.

Up the steps he leapt, two at a time. Inside the front office, a desk sergeant and a constable looked up in amazement as the weighty file zig-zagged through the air towards them. Directly in front of the sergeant, the file seemed to stop . . . hover. Then Tim raised it slowly, slowly, into the air . . . *and brought it down with a hefty wallop on the police sergeant's head*!

"WAAAOOW." Before the man had time to recover, Invisible Tim turned and raced outside again, still clutching the all-important secret file.

"W-Wilkins, did you see what happened . . .?"

"Yes, Sarge, I *did*," said the constable grimly. "Come on, let's get *after* that thing — whatever it is."

Tim, meanwhile, had raced back along the street towards the oncoming Phil and Laurie. When they saw the file floating back towards them, they stopped, gasped, pointed. Before they could say anything, Tim lobbed the file neatly into the shaking hands of big Phil.

It was just then, that the police sergeant and his constable came pelting round the corner.

"Strewth, it's the *law*," said Laurie weakly. "We've got the file again, so let's scarper." And turning on their heels, the two men fled.

It was a short and undramatic chase. Already exhausted by their initial exertions, Phil and Laurie proved no match for the pursuing policemen. They were halted only a few yards from their parked car, whose number the alert young constable took special note of. Invisible Tim, watching nearby,

The file came down with a wallop on the police sergeant's head.

was delighted when the car proved to be stolen. That made the police sergeant even more interested in the mysterious file, and a series of telephone calls to the Talbot house soon revealed what had happened. Laurie and Phil were promptly arrested and charged.

LATE HOME!

AFTER making himself visible again, Tim, unfortunately, had to make his own way home by a series of erratic 'bus journeys. He arrived home just after midnight, more than a little weary and a month's pocket money worse off. His father was still being interviewed by a senior police officer when Tim lurched in through the door. Mr Talbot looked up and blinked. "Tim," he said with a note of surprise in his voice. "I'm afraid I'd forgotten all

about you. We've had some tremendous excitement here this evening."

"Yes, a policeman at the front door has told me all about it," lied Tim benignly.

"Oh! In that case I won't bore you with the details again," said Mr Talbot. "Weren't you saying something earlier about going for fish and chips? You can toddle off now if you like."

"Thanks a lot, Dad, but I think you'll find that the chippy closed an hour and a half ago." Tim lowered himself into a chair and smiled gently at the ceiling. "I shouldn't really expect any *thanks* for what I did tonight," he thought. "Not even fish and chips. My power is a secret and that's that. There again, I *am* the Invisible Boy. If the fat at the chippy is still hot, maybe I can climb through a window and *cook* myself some . . ."

The illustration shows two pictures of the same jar. In the first, the jar contains a lump of something. But, in the second the 'lump' is gone. In real life, how could you make this vanishing trick happen without touching the jar once the lump is in it?

PENNY POSER

Put penny (3) between pennies (1) and (2) without touching penny (1) or shifting penny (2).

CARD CARVE-UP

Three playing cards were each cut into three pieces. Eight of the pieces are shown here. One piece is missing. From which card in the pack was the missing piece cut?

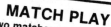

EYE TEST

Without using a ruler or a set square, decide whether the square set in the series of circles is a perfect one.

MATCH PLAY

Remove two matches and leave behind only two squares, of different sizes.

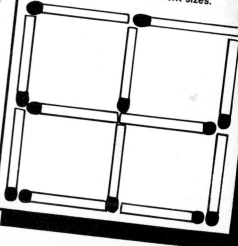

FORM A CROSS

Trace or copy the shape four times. Cut them out and then arrange them, without any overlapping, to form a cross.

WHAT ARE THEY

Here are a couple of familiar objects photographed in close-up. If you can recognise them quickly then you're certainly on the ball!

The L2A3 shown with butt folded

EAGLE

STERLING L2A3 MACHINE GUN

THE L2A3 is the standard submachine gun for the army and was seen recently carried by British troops during the Falklands campaign. New Zealand, Canada, India and several other countries have adopted it for their armies and there is also a special version which is issued to some police forces.

It was developed by G. W. Patchett at the Sterling Engineering Company in Essex during World War Two, but it was not officially adopted until the early fifties when it became known as the Sterling. Since its adoption, the weapon has gone through several modifications in its long life, finally resulting in the L2A3.

Facelift

Overall it shows many improvements over the old Sten Gun. Sharp grooves on the outer surface of the bolt on the Sterling act as a cleaning device to cut away any dirt or grit in the receiver. Also, rollers are fitted to the magazine follower which reduces friction and allows the ammunition to feed smoothly through the breech. A knife type bayonet can be fitted to the L2A3 and the stock can be folded so it is easier to carry when not in use. By simply pushing a lever the marksman has a choice of either fully automatic fire or thirty four single shots.

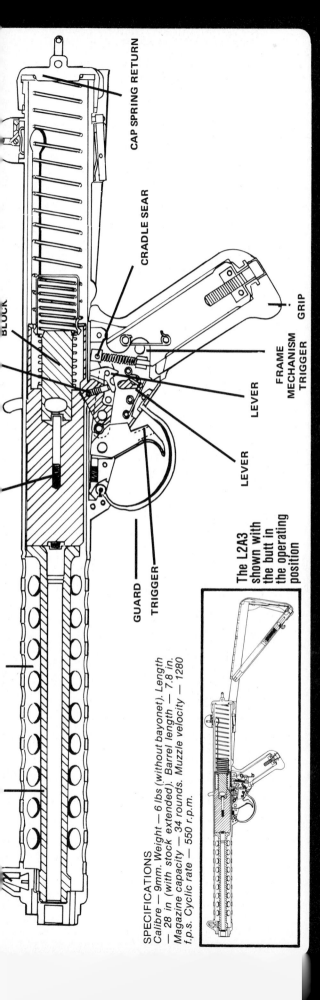

SPECIFICATIONS
Calibre — 9mm. Weight — 6 lbs (without bayonet). Length — 28 in (with stock extended). Barrel length — 7.8 in. Magazine capacity — 34 rounds. Muzzle velocity — 1280 f.p.s. Cyclic rate — 550 r.p.m.

The L2A3 shown with the butt in the operating position

BIG MOUTH

Here are some of Lenny Henry's answers to readers' letters taken from his ever-bulging postbag sent in to EAGLE weekly.

HEY, MIND MY BIKE!

How come old ladies always get in my way when I ride my bicycle home on the pavement at nights? I can't ride on the road because it's too dangerous, especially as I haven't got lights. As soon as I get up a burst of speed, some old dear comes hobbling round the corner, and then we're both on our backsides glaring at each other. What can I do to avoid this situation?
Roger, Manchester.
You nasty little brat, Roger! Algernon Razzmatazz is putting you in his book of people he least wants to meet. Take a tip, kid, leave your bike at home!

BIG IS BEAUTIFUL

Do you think big families are better than small ones? I have only one sister, but my friend has four older brothers, six sisters, eight cousins, ten aunts and 12 uncles. At Christmas and birthdays he gets more presents than I'll get in a lifetime. And you should see the load of Easter Eggs that he receives!
Wallace, Blackpool.
Presents aren't everything, Wally! There's love, kindness . . . and say what happens to your friend's surplus Easter Eggs? Tell him that all that chocolate will make him fat and that you would be only too pleased to help him avoid becoming a Billy Bunter!

SKELETON IN THE CLOSET

While on half-term holiday, I decided to look up my family history and found that I was directly descended from a notorious crook who trained boys to be thieves, just like Fagin in *Oliver Twist* by Charles Dickens.

As they say that blood is stronger than water, does this mean that I have inherited his evil ways? I often worry about this, although I have not broken the law yet. But if I did, would it be my fault, or would it be my evil ancestor acting through me?
Hamish, Glasgow.
Trevor Macdoughnut laughed his head off when he read this letter. Evil influences from the past can't possibly affect you, can they? No distant ancestor could make you break the law if you did not want to! Nooo waaay!

B·1B
Strategic Air Command's new strength

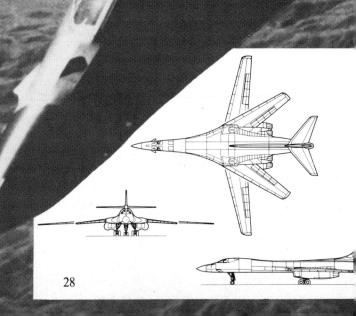

The new B-1B long-range combat aircraft is to replace part of the ageing fleet of B-52 bombers which form the third element of America's Triad of Strategic Defenses. The other elements in the U.S. three-pronged defence force are land-based intercontinental ballistic missiles and submarine-launched ballistic missiles.

One hundred B-1B's have been ordered and the company responsible for building them, *Rockwell International*, have announced that the first will roll off the production line in late 1984. The B-1B is America's most advanced military aircraft, able to fly greater distances on less fuel, with a higher payload of weapons and with a lower risk of detection by enemy radar.

The old B-52 bombers are heavy and rely on aerial refuelling. Also, because it is a fixed-wing aircraft, the B-52's speed when flying at high or low altitudes is limited which means it can be spotted more easily by enemy radar equipment. The B-1B has swing wings which, when in the full-forward position, allow it to take off quickly from relatively small airfields. For high subsonic operations or low level penetrations, the wings are changed to the full-swept position.

Skimming the tree-tops at only 200 feet the B-1B has its own terrain-following radar system while the enemy equipment would find it hard to differentiate between the aircraft and the surrounding mountains, trees, buildings, etc.

Pay-load!

The plane's sophisticated electronic counter-measures (ECM), flares and manoeuvrability allow it to detect or defeat surface-to-air missiles, enemy aircraft and anti-aircraft artillery.

The B-1B has three weapons' bays plus the facilities for carrying fuel and weapons externally on the underside of the fuselage. The two forward bays have a movable bulkhead so nuclear air-to-ground missiles, including 14 Cruise missiles, conventional and nuclear gravity bombs and additional fuel can be easily accommodated. Whereas the B-52 needs a crew of six, the B-1B only requires four and they, plus their equipment, are shielded from the deadly rays of nuclear explosions.

This versatile aircraft is not just designed as an attacker, it will also be used for long-range sea surveillance, long-range anti-submarine patrol and aerial mine laying.

The B-1B will be powered by four giant General Electric F101-GE-102 turbofan engines (30,000-pound thrust class) as seen in the picture below. These will allow the aircraft to travel at subsonic speeds at high or low altitudes and fly at a maximum operating weight of 477,000 pounds.

...BUT I DO WANT HIM STUFFED.

STUFFED! NOW HOLD ON A MINUTE, LADY...

IT MUST BE DONE BY MISTER HENDERSON, A DEAR FRIEND—WHO LIVES IN SCOTLAND. AND MISTER PROSSER MUST BE THERE BY MIDDAY TOMORROW OR HE WON'T BE ABLE TO WORK ON HIM...

I CAN'T GO MYSELF—YOU'RE MY ONLY HOPE, MISTER SOPER. I'LL PAY YOU SEVENTY POUNDS... PLUS EXPENSES.

TAKING A DEAD CAT TO BE STUFFED... HARDLY HIGH-CLASS DETECTIVE WORK, IS IT?

BUT, THEN AGAIN, WHAT WOULD I KNOW ABOUT HIGH-CLASS DETECTIVE WORK...

BESIDES, OTHER PEOPLE WERE ABOUT TO TAKE AN INTEREST AND THEY DEFINITELY WEREN'T ANIMAL LOVERS...

YOU MUST'VE IMAGINED IT, JOE. WHY WOULD A BIG GREY CAR TRAIL YOU FROM MRS WHITES? FORGET IT. PACK YOUR BAG AND SHOOT TO SCOTLAND FOR THAT CASH...

BUT THAT WAS GOING TO BE EASIER SAID THAN DONE...

HEY— WHO PUT THAT LOCK ON MY BIKE?

IT LOOKS LIKE SOMEONE DOESN'T WANT ME TO MAKE THIS SCOTTISH TRIP!

STILL, I'M NOT WAITING TO FIND OUT WHY!

HEY, YOU! COME BACK HERE..!

...BEFORE I TRAVELLED TO THE STATION!

ALL I NEED NOW IS MY TICKET...

I'M NOT A BETTING MAN BUT I'LL LAY TWO TO ONE THOSE GUYS PUT MY BIKE OUT OF ACTION!

WELL DONE, LONDON TRANSPORT! BUT I DON'T GET IT — WHAT CAN BE SO IMPORTANT ABOUT ME OR A DEAD CAT..?

I DECIDED TO TAKE A PRECAUTION OR TWO...

AND ONE WEEKEND RETURN TO SCOTLAND LATER...

PLATFORM FIVE THE TICKET MAN SAID...

JUST A SECOND, SOPER..!

32

JUST ONE PROBLEM... WHERE'S THE TRAIN?

I DON'T UNDERSTAND... IT WAS NEVER LIKE THIS FOR GENE HACKMAN!

OF COURSE, I WAS FORGETTING... MY NAME IS JOE SOAP.

AND NOTHING EVER WORKS QUITE RIGHT FOR ME...

C-CAN'T KEEP... THIS UP FOR MUCH LONGER! GOTTA STOP... AND HIDE!

A PHOTO BOOTH SEEMED JUST THE PLACE. BUT I'D FORGOTTEN THE JOE SOAP LUCK!

PARDON ME, MISS... BUT I-I JUST HAD TO... JOIN YOU...

OH, YES... I UNDERSTAND...

TRUST ME TO STUMBLE IN UPON THE BIGGEST MAN-HUNTER SINCE JAWS!

COME TO THINK OF IT, SHE MIGHT HAVE ACTUALLY BEEN JAWS.

LADY, I THINK I'D RATHER TAKE MY CHANCES WITH THE TWO HEAVIES!

COME BACK, LOVER BOY! COME BACK!

LUCKILY, I COULD OUTRUN HOT LIPS AND THE OTHER TWO SEEMED TO HAVE DISAPPEARED

34

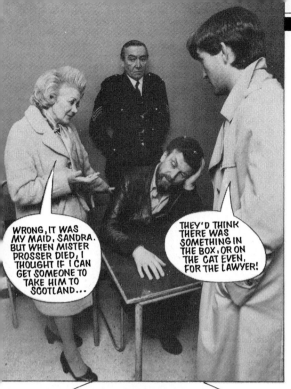

WRONG, IT WAS MY MAID, SANDRA. BUT WHEN MISTER PROSSER DIED, I THOUGHT IF I CAN GET SOMEONE TO TAKE HIM TO SCOTLAND...

THEY'D THINK THERE WAS SOMETHING IN THE BOX, OR ON THE CAT EVEN, FOR THE LAWYER!

RIGHT! I DISCOVERED IT WAS SANDRA WHEN I HEARD HER TELEPHONING PETER, TELLING HIM TO PUT SOME MEN ON TO YOU, JOE...

THE TWO HEAVIES! I SUPPOSE YOU HANDED HER OVER TO THE POLICE WHILE YOU CAME UP HERE...!

I WAS LEFT WITH THE DISTINCT FEELING THAT I HADN'T DONE TOO WELL...

LIKE THE CAT SAID WHEN HE LICKED HIS SHAVED LEG... IT JUST AIN'T FUR!

WRONG AGAIN! I LEFT HER IN THE HANDS OF CONNORS, MY BUTLER, TO KEEP HER AWAY FROM PETER, WHILE I CAME NORTH. SHE DID IT ALL FOR LOVE, YOU SEE, AND I DIDN'T WANT TO TURN HER OVER TO THE POLICE FOR THAT.

JUST ABOUT EVERYBODY SEEMED TO UNDERSTAND THIS CASE BETTER THAN I DID.

STILL, PUSS, AT LEAST I CAME OUT OF IT IN ONE PIECE...

YOU AGAIN! AND UP TO YOUR OLD TRICKS, TOO!

WHY DO I SAY THINGS LIKE THAT..?

WELL, JUST LEAVE THAT POOR PUSSY ALONE!

YAAARRGH!

ANOTHER CASE OVER – ANOTHER JOE SOAP CATASTROPHE!

THE END

SADDLE TRAMP

recalls the story of

SHOOT-OUT AT YELLOW BEND

The Wild West was a vast, untamed land where good folk often needed protection for themselves and their families from the unlawful. Me — I chose dollars earned from a bounty reward as my kind of justice. But some men did not need the lure of money to see that justice was done — not if they had a burning desire for vengeance. Such a man was Indian chief Big Feather. . .

A bullet whined through the air and both men drew their guns, ready for the fray. "Darn Indians," spat Chuck.

" 'Tain't right, nohow," grunted Pop Wheeler, as he shot a stream of yellow liquid into the spittoon on the floor of the Red Canyon Saloon. "No, sir," he added, chewing at his plug of 'baccy.

"You sound as angry as a rattlesnake," chuckled the bartender, pouring Pop another shot of bourbon.

"Why, I sure am," snorted Pop. "Here's these two young fellows aiming to ride over the hills to Yellow Bend Township — and everybody from here to Nevada knows that the hills are full of murderous Redskins. I wouldn't give much for your chances, fellers. Nope, I sure wouldn't!"

The two men he was talking about just laughed. They were both tough-looking guys with tanned, leathery faces and sharp, shifty eyes.

One winked at the other and said in a drawl, "Reckon I've got a bullet that's a mite faster than any Redskin's arrow."

"Pardner," growled Pop. "You sound so drawly, I guess any Red-

38

Fearlessly flinging himself from his horse to recover his gun, the Indian gave a war whoop of defiance. Vengeance burned in his eyes.

skin's arrow would plug you while you were snoring on your horse."

It was a mistake to say that, as Pop found out. The glass he was holding was shattered by a bullet, which tore through it and smashed the large mirror behind the bar. More bullets began splintering floorboards at Pop's feet, making him dance like a Dervish to avoid them.

"Hey!" shouted Pop, quivering like a jelly. "Ain't no call to get angry."

"We ain't angry," answered the men, their guns still smoking. "We're just havin' fun."

With a wide sweep of his arm, one of the men brushed all the glasses and bottles from the bar, causing them to fall to the floor with a shattering clatter. Laughing, the man jumped on to the bar and jeered at the drinkers and gamblers.

"Ain't nobody gonna get hurt if they do what I say," he shouted. "My pal Chuck is a friendly guy. He's coming round to collect your gold, dollar bills, watches and any other valuables you've got. Pop them into his hat, okay?"

Ambush

"I'll see you in Hell first," bellowed a big rancher from the back.

A bullet sang through the air, the rancher's hat flew off and a red line streaked his forehead. With a startled look fixed on his face, and his eyes glazed, the rancher slid to the floor.

"Ain't nobody been known to disagree with me and live," shouted the man, slipping his revolver back into its holster.

In glum silence, the gamblers and drinkers handed over their valuables, and Chuck and his pal felt that they were on to a good thing. They did not see that the bartender had escaped through the back door and called the sheriff. But they knew when the saloon's swing doors burst inward and the sheriff stood there, his hands resting on the six-shooters at his hips.

"Drop that gun," he yelled to the gangster on the bar, "or I'll. . ."

He didn't get a chance to finish his sentence. His gun spun from his hand, the target of a well-aimed shot from the man on the bar. Simultaneously, Chuck put a shot through the swinging oil lamp. It crashed to the floor and soon flames began licking at the floorboards.

To avoid the inevitable inferno, the gamblers and bankers began scrambling madly to get out of the saloon. Under cover of the panic, Chuck and his pal escaped with their loot on to their horses hitched on a post outside. They fled to the hills in the darkness of the night. When dawn came they had ridden far through rocky, mountain passes and along dusty, waggon-

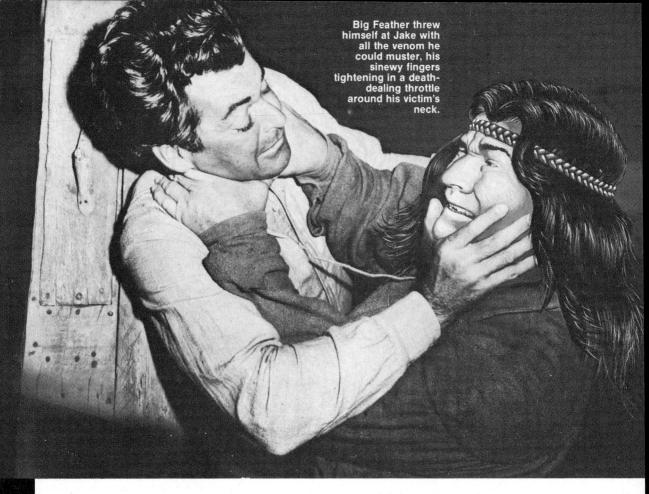

Big Feather threw himself at Jake with all the venom he could muster, his sinewy fingers tightening in a death-dealing throttle around his victim's neck.

rutted tracks.

"I reckon there'll be rich pickings in Yellow Bend Township," said Jake, for that was the name of Chuck's partner.

Chuck chuckled. "Them drinkers and gamblers sure do hand over their dough easy."

"Horsefeed," said Jake with a curse. "I'm after somethin' bigger'n that."

"The bank?" queried Chuck.

"Too right," agreed Jake. "And I ain't aimin' to write no cheques, neither."

Chuckling, the men rode on their way.

Ever since the white man had driven the Indians out of the rich grazing lands of the West, bands of Indians had haunted the hills and plains, and they hated the white man. So it's no wonder that there was blood lust in the hearts of the group of Redskins who sat on their horses silhouetted against the sky on a hilltop. Below them in the valley rode the two bandits.

Silently, the Indians rode down the hill under the cover of rocky cliffs.

By now the trail was winding through rock-strewn territory, with a few scrubby trees. Ahead of the men, around a bend, two rocks stood like sentinels on either side of the trail. As the men were about to pass between these rocks, the crack of a report echoed among the hills. A bullet whined through the air, ricocheting off one of the rocks.

Instinctively, the men whirled in their saddles, just in time to see a feathered head drop behind a boulder up the hill.

"Darn Indians," spat Chuck, jumping off his horse. Crouching and using the animal as a shield, he fired at the Indian in the hills. Volley after volley of lead streamed on to Jake and Chuck. In desperation, they remounted and headed for the only cover of Sentinel Rocks.

Hostage

Just in time, they caught a glimpse of the Indians waiting there to ambush them, and wrenched their horses round. After them came the Indians on their fleet-footed ponies, their rifles spitting lead and venom.

Turning in the saddle and firing, Chuck shot the leading Indian's gun from his hand, and the Indian fearlessly flung himself from his horse to recover it. Regaining his gun, he fired from a prone position on the ground.

The battle was furious, but the more accurate fire of the white men was in their favour. Before long, all of the Indians had fled to nurse their wounds. Only one remained — their leader, Big Feather.

Vengeance burned in the Indian's brown eyes as he looked at his captors.

"Reckon I'll take you along with me as a hostage, Injun," said Chuck. "Don't reckon your pals will bother us so long as they figure I'm gonna plug you at the first sign of trouble. Now get on your horse and lead us to Yellow Bend Township. We've got an appointment at a banking house in that town.

For all its grand name, the Yellow Bend Township Banking House was nothing more than a wooden shack, and its cash in an iron safe. It was early morning and banker Spike Murphy was counting out the dollars he'd need to pay to the cowhands of the ranches thereabouts later that day. Neatly piled on the table before him was a fortune in dollar bills.

"Hands up, banker!" Spike Murphy's hand flew for the Smith & Wesson in his desk drawer. But he was dead before he reached it, with a neat hole drilled in his forehead.

"Easy pickin's, like I said," chuckled Jake, coming into the bank with his smoking gun, followed by Chuck, whose Colt was rammed into Big Feather's ribs.

Grabbing a leather bag from the

floor, Jake began cramming the mounds of dollar bills into it. Big Feather's eyes were darting from one to the other, and suddenly he saw his chance.

At the instance that Jake tossed the filled bag to Chuck, Big Feather was not covered by any of their guns. Like a demon, he flew out of the bank giving war whoops bloodcurling enough to raise the dead — or at least, the sheriff. Then he turned and threw himself at Jake with all the venom he could summon, his sinewy fingers tightening in a death-dealing throttle around his victim's neck.

In fear of his life, Chuck shot out of the bank and on to his horse. But too late, around the bend came the sheriff and posse, firing as their horses skidded into the town square. Their guns spat fire and Chuck bit the dust, dying, as he always said he would, in the saddle.

In the bank, Jake was pleading for Big Feather to show mercy.

"Okay, Injun," grunted the sheriff. "Let 'im go. Reckon we'll give him a fair trial, then string him up! Guess our townsfolk owe you a heap of gratitude for what you did today."

Big Feather smiled with pleasure. "Bad men," he said. "Indians not like bad men."

"Reckon that goes for white folk as well," grinned the sheriff. "Shake, pardner!"

Big Feather did so, and then rode to rejoin his people in the hills, happy to think that justice had been done.

THE END

EAGLE Interviews... LENNY BENNETT

They say that making people laugh is the hardest job in show business, but here we meet someone who makes it look so simple. . . top comic LENNY BENNETT!

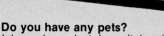

Which comics did you read when you were a boy, Lenny?
I certainly read the old EAGLE, with the adventures of Dan Dare in it. "Champion" was another of my favourites. In that comic, the stories were all told in words rather than pictures.

Were you a great comic reader?
Yes, I was. When I was a boy, there was hardly any television. Also, there was not so much material around to read. Of course, the contents of the comics were far more mundane than they are today.

How about hobbies? What are your favourites?
I am a fitness fanatic. I've run in the New York marathon. I also took part in the London marathon in 1982 and completed it in three hours and 26 minutes. Squash is another of my favourites. I've always been interested in sport, and I've played football and boxed for my country.

If you were not in show business, what would you like to be doing?
I'd be a journalist. I was one for seven years for a local Blackpool evening newspaper. I started off as a junior reporter and finished up writing articles about show business. However, I got rather fed up with that. I used to write jokes for people and then I started writing them for myself. And that's how I got into the world of show business.

How did hosting the "Punchlines" TV series suit you?
Very well! It was a series that was great fun to do. And the first show of the last series went out on Christmas Eve, which was lovely!

Who is your favourite show business personality?
W C Fields, the famous comedian, who was a star before most EAGLE readers were born. However, my current favourites are Richard Pryor, Les Dawson and Jimmy Tarbuck.

Do you have any pets?
I love dogs, but I can't have one because I'm travelling all the time. I really like labradors and retrievers.

Have you a favourite food?
Hot curries. Apart from that, I like very simple food.

What sort of car do you drive?
A Mercedes 500 SEL.

Have you any musical favourites?
I like all kinds of music, but my favourite singer is Elkie Brooks.

Embarrassing moments. . . have there been any of these?
Yes, when I was beaten at squash by a 72-year-old man. He was brilliant — and a former heavyweight boxer. I finished up as a heap in the corner after that game!

What are your plans for the future?
To survive!
And keep joking to the end, eh, Lenny?

BUILD A BATTLEFIELD!

With a little effort, this is what your battlefield will look like. It was made by a model-maker, using Airfix kits. See if you can make a battle as realistic as this one. Below, is a close-up of the battlefield which shows the incredible detail that can be achieved.

Your battlefield can be as good as the one shown here, if you follow the simple rules below. It was made by a professional model-maker and shows four US marines advancing across a clearing in the WWII Pacific zone.

1 Study your subject carefully before you begin work. Public libraries and museums will help you with this. Look for books with pictures of uniforms, and other equipment.

2 Decide how many soldiers you will have on your battlefield. If this is small, three or four men should be sufficient. Too many fighters will make the setting look cluttered.

3 Take your time in posing the figures and deciding where to put them. Two men with identical poses will look awkward, so make them different. Look in a mirror to see how *you* sit, stand, lean, walk, run and fall.

4 Remember that men, even when they are carrying heavy equipment, stand on the ground and not in it, so don't sink boots into the surface.

5 If your figures are running, walking or throwing a grenade, they will look if they are tilted slightly off balance. This gives a sense of movement. Heads should gaze in a specific direction, and sitting figures look natural when bent at the waist.

6 Equipment worn by soldiers (such as packs and webbing) sags and moulds itself to the wearer's shape. So make sure these things fit the man naturally and comfortably.

7 During combat, shoulder-arms and other hand-held weapons are gripped tightly. Fit these in the correct firing positions.

8 When painting your figures, make them look as though they are fighting in dust, sand or mud. On the battlefield, uniforms and equipment soon get faded and soiled, and men weatherbeaten.

9 Keep your battlefield simple. Too many trees and buildings will look confusing and possibly hide too many of your figures. If you wish, improve the setting in stages.

10 Your soldiers should be doing something relevant to the battle. Some men might be firing or taking cover, while others might be wounded or reloading weapons. The men will look better if they are placed diagonally instead of facing directly to the left or right.

Stuck for some poses for your soldiers? Here are some drawings to give you an idea. With a multi-pose kit, you can arrange your figures any way you want.

43

WHAT TO DO:

1: Doomlord — the dread servitor of Nox — is on Earth to pass judgement on its people. Impress the awesome alien by outsmarting him in this challenge quiz.

2: There are 30 questions, each with a choice of three alternative answers. Every question is connected with space or science fiction. Try to answer correctly as many questions as you can.

3: Each correct answer is hidden somewhere in the word search grid. It can be written vertically, horizontally, diagonally, backwards or forwards — but always in a straight line, with no letters being missed. (One answer is ringed as an example — reads backwards PLUTO). So, if you don't know all the answers right away, you can work them out using the word search. Good luck!

1. Who recorded the song 'Space Oddity' . . . Dollar, Bowie or Toyah?

2. In which film did Darth Vader appear . . . 'Star Wars', 'Logan's Run' or 'Raiders Of The Lost Ark'?

3. What is the name of Dan Dare's dreaded foe . . . Khan, Timelord or Mekon?

4. The scientific study of the stars and planets . . . is known as . . . astrology, astronomy or ptolemy?

5. Which of these planets is farthest away from Earth . . . Mars, Jupiter or Neptune?

6. Who wrote the novel 2001 . . . H.G. Wells, George Lucas or Arthur C. Clarke?

7. Can you name the first servitor Doomlord to arrive on this planet: Was his name . . . Zyn, Nog or Xen?

8. When a star explodes is it said to go . . . inferno, starstruck or supernova?

9. Who presents the popular TV series 'The Sky At Night' . . . Noel Edmunds, Patrick Moore or Raymond Baxter?

10. Where would you find the Sea of Clouds, the Sea of Crises and the Ocean of Storms . . . Moon, Jupiter or Mars?

11. In John Wyndham's novel, what was the name of the murderous plants . . . Wallflowers, Triffids or Spiderplants?

I am Doomlord. The future of the entire human race is in my hands. Do you dare, puny human, to accept my quiz challenge?

12. Distance in space is spoken of in terms of _____ years. Is the missing word . . . leap, light or black?

13. Who was the first Earthman to walk on the Moon . . . Aldrin, Armstrong or Sting?

14. Who sang about a 'Rocket Man' . . . Captain Sensible, Bad Manners or Elton John?

15. In 'Star Trek', was the name of the exploration craft . . . Enterprise, Orbiter or Spock?

16. Which planet is the nearest of all to Earth . . . Venus, Saturn or Mercury?

17. What is the name of the alien editor of the sci-fi comic 2000AD . . . Tharg, Rumpelstiltskin or Quarxis?

18. Luke _____ appeared in the film 'Star Wars'. What was his second name . . . Hammill, Skywalker or Gronk?

19. What is the term for a strange, unexplained object sighted in the sky . . . UFO, ESP or CIA?

20. An exact duplicate of someone or something is called a . . . clone, copycat or look-alike?

21. Earth's new re-usable space craft is called the . . . shuttle, telecom or satellite?

22. Dan Dare's famous ancestor was accompanied on his adventures by . . . Manix, Plumduff or Digby?

23. 'Stainless Steel _____'. Which word completes the title of Harry Harrison's book . . . Sink, Rat or Thief?

24. Only one planet in the Solar System has just a single moon. Is that planet . . . Uranus, Jupiter or Earth?

25. Movement of objects in the heavens sometimes results in one object being obscured from view by Earth. Is this known as an . . . eclipse, extra-terrestrial or accidental?

26. What is the name of Dr Who's time and space travelling policebox . . . Tiswas, Tardis or Tardelli?

27. Between Jupiter and Mars there are countless lumps of rock. Are they known as asteroids, debris or rock 'n' roll?

28. Is Seki-lines the name of a . . . space sickness, comet or fictional alien airline?

29. Which country launched the Apollo space crafts . . . USA, USSR or Australia?

30. One planet shares the same name as a Walt Disney cartoon character. Is that planet . . . Saturn, Mercury or Pluto?

Do not incur DOOMLORD's wrath and look at the answers below before completing the Quiz. When you have completed it, this Word Search grid has all the 30 answers hidden in it. Can you find them?

A	R	T	H	U	R	C	C	L	A	R	K	E	I
R	S	T	A	R	W	A	R	S	V	X	U	H	C
R	T	A	E	A	R	T	H	O	T	F	L	E	E
E	O	E	S	N	R	H	U	N	T	O	N	C	
K	Y	U	R	O	C	A	T	R	N	U	V	L	
L	A	S	N	O	E	R	T	E	T	E	L	I	
A	H	O	M	M	I	G	L	P	N	T	I	P	
W	M	E	W	F	W	D	E	U	P	A	G	S	
Y	T	P	F	N	O	N	S	S	E	R	H	E	
K	Z	I	O	Y	B	G	I	D	T	D	T	A	
S	D	K	E	N	T	E	R	P	R	I	S	E	
S	E	L	T	O	N	J	O	H	N	S	I	G	
M	E	R	O	O	M	K	C	I	R	T	A	P	

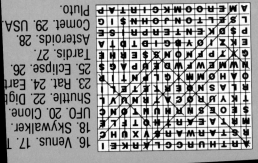

THE POWERBOAT
SPEEDMASTER ON WATER!

1. Anti-torque break-away steering. 2. Brake switch. 3. Switch-panel: starter and fuel pump, prime, engine raise and lower, kill switch. 4. Sling mounting brackets. 5. Detachable front bodywork. 6. Fuel tank. 7. Compressed air bottles for brakes. 8. Stringers. 9. Bulkhead. 10. Sponson. 11. Fuel line. 12. Fuel filter. 13. Fuel pump. 14. Fuel flow control valve. 15. Hydraulic trim pump. 16. Master switch. 17. Transom. 18. Steering bar. 19. Inspection cover. 20. Drain bung. 21. Brake. 22. Detachable rear bodywork. 23. 3.5 litre V8 engine. 24. 'Cleaver' propeller.

HITTING the water at 150km/h is like hitting concrete! But that is what can happen to a driver in the John Player Special powerboat. When trouble strikes, the driver tugs at a jack plug which stops the engines, inflates his lifejacket and sends him flying clear of the boat. This safety device is essential because the streamlined, plywood catamaran hurtles across the water, scarcely touching the surface under the power of its huge 3.5 litre outboard motor. Since the first powerboat series in 1975, winning speeds in waterborne Grand Prix racing have increased and the John Player three-boat team have been meeting tough competition. Driving skill is the keynote and careful trimming is vital in maintaining control. The engine is tilted in and out hydraulically to alter the angle between the hull and the surface. Trim too high and air can get under the tunnel hull and blow the boat over on its back. Trim too low and the boat may dig a sponson in the water and hook round, throwing the driver through the cockpit cowling.

46

DAN DARE
Pilot of the Future

MOONBASE *ENJOYSVILLE*. A FANTASTIC DOMED CITY ON THE SURFACE OF THE MOON...

HERE, WEARY SPACE TRAVELLERS COULD FIND REST, FUN AND RELAXATION...

DAN DARE, GREAT-GREAT GRANDSON OF THE LEGENDARY SPACE HERO... AND NOW A HERO IN HIS OWN RIGHT... WAS NEARING *ENJOYSVILLE*...

WELCOME TO MOON ORBIT. YOUR RESERVATION AT MOONBASE ENJOYSVILLE HAS BEEN NOTED. ALL PREPARATIONS ARE IN HAND. HAVE A NICE DAY.

DON'T WORRY, COMPUTER. I'LL HAVE A NICE DAY, NICE WEEK, NICE MONTH.

DAN'S VICTORY OVER *THE MEKON* HAD MADE HIM AN INTERNATIONAL CELEBRITY. THERE WAS AN OFFICIAL WELCOME FOR HIM...

YOU ARE OUR HONOURED GUEST, MISTER DARE. IF THERE'S ANYTHING WE CAN DO...

CUT OUT THE SPECIAL TREATMENT FOR A START. I JUST WANT TO RELAX IN PEACE...

...I ONLY SAVED THE WHOLE WORLD, NOTHING MORE!

AND DAN DID RELAX. FIRST IN THE ANTI-GRAV PAVILION...

THIS IS THE LIFE... JUST FLOATING AROUND, DOING NOTHING!

49

50

WHAT'S GOING ON? WHO NEEDS RESCUING?

IT'S COMING STRAIGHT FOR ME!

THE JET-PACK ON DAN'S BACK SAVED HIS LIFE!

GOT TO... DESTROY DARE! IT... HAS... BEEN ORDERED!

THIS TIME, THE CRAFT WAS VERY CLOSE TO DAN...

...CLOSE ENOUGH FOR HIM TO GRAB A HOLD, AS IT WENT PAST...

GOT IT!

FROM THERE, IT WAS AN EASY MATTER TO OPEN THE SMALL AIRLOCK, AND TUMBLE INSIDE...

53

54

'Reckon you would like to be an enquiry agent like me? Try tackling these questions and see how you would have reacted when out on a case!'

1. You're sitting in your office when at five to six in walks a Chinaman carrying a tray of take away food. He says he has no money to pay for your services, but he has something 'hot' that needs your instant atten-tion. What do you do?
A) Decide that the office is closed.
B) Ask him to explain what's going on.
C) Say you'll listen if he gives you a plate of prawn chow mein.

2. The man is a new waiter at the Red Dragon restaurant. He opens a container marked 'Chef special rice' and it's stashed with cash! This is part of an order to be collected by a

HOW GOOD A JOE SOAP ARE YOU?

customer in a few minutes. The worried waiter suspects something sinister. What do you do?
A) Go to the Red Dragon and ang-rily demand a fresh portion of rice.
B) Instruct the waiter to return to the restaurant and let the food be collected.
C) Tell the waiter to see the manager.

3. In the Red Dragon you are study-ing the menu when two people come in, both to collect take away food. How do you find out which one will be given the package con-taining the loot?
A) Confront the two people with the fact that you know that one of them has really come to pick up some cash.
B) Pretend to trip over so you can 'accidentally' break open both sets of take away food.
C) Claim that the package with 'Chef special rice' is really for you and demand to know which of them has taken it.

4. The container of cash went to someone who comes from the Star of India restaurant. You decided that you must get into the kitchens of the Indian restaurant. But how?
A) Sneak in through the back window.
B) Go through the restaurant and pretend to be a health inspector making a late-night call.
C) Attack the waiter in the street and take his place, hoping no-one will notice the difference.

5. You are safely in the kitchens, hidden from the kitchen staff by some huge sacks of curry powder. Suddenly, you realise that the curry powder is going to make you sneeze. Do you. . .?
A) Try to get away with the old 'I'm-trying-to-find-the-Gents' trick, or vinderloo as the Indians say. (Find the loo. Get it?)
B) Grab a nearby chipattie, and cover your face to muffle the noise.
C) Sneeze and then run for it.

6. Later on, you are watching the outside of the Star of India when the Chinese waiter who got you into this sweet and sour situation, comes out carrying a bag of take away food. What is your course of action?
A) Ask him what he's up to.
B) Pretend you found the bag lying in the street and accidentally disco-vered the cash.
C) Keep the cash and refuse to return it until you get a satisfactory explanation.

7. You discover that the Red Dragon manager told the new waiter to go and collect a 'Chef special' from the Indian restaurant. And, yes, there's a wodge of cash stashed in one of the containers. You decide that you will personally deliver this parcel to the Red Dragon manager. How will you go about this?
A) Call in, say who you are and

Continued on page 74

55

GET KARTING-1

Records have crumbled under the singing tyres of the Zip-Hermetite super-karting team. With their 250cc racer (left and above), they have won every major championship throughout the world. Among their trophies they number the premier event in Britain, the Hermetite Grand Prix. At this, some 400 karters fight for four GP titles.

The first woman to figure in a top kart team is Carolynn Grant Sale (far right) of the Zip-Hermetites. With her is the leader, Martin Hines (centre) and Simon Mercer. Superkarts are capable of speeds up to 145mph and racing on the full length circuits is restricted to drivers over 17.

Aerodynamically styled for speed, the 250cc superkarts tear round the track with their drivers a mere fraction of an inch the tarmac. Compared with formula racing, Superkarting atively cheap. . . but it's also fast. You can start racing our eleventh birthday with a small kart for around £500. those in our pictures are quality cars costing thousands.

BRRR! THE DAYS ARE GETTING COLD!

THOSE LITTLE BIRDS HAVE GOT THE RIGHT IDEA, THEY'RE MIGRATING TO A COUNTRY WITH A WARMER CLIMATE. I THINK I'LL DO THE SAME.

GOODBYE, ROOF OF KING'S REACH TOWER — I'M OFF ON A VERY LONG JOURNEY!

YOU DIDN'T THINK I WAS GOING TO FLY ALL THE WAY THERE, DID YOU?

BUS STOP

57

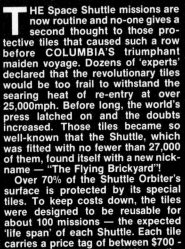

THE Space Shuttle missions are now routine and no-one gives a second thought to those protective tiles that caused such a row before COLUMBIA'S triumphant maiden voyage. Dozens of 'experts' declared that the revolutionary tiles would be too frail to withstand the searing heat of re-entry at over 25,000mph. Before long, the world's press latched on and the doubts increased. Those tiles became so well-known that the Shuttle, which was fitted with no fewer than 27,000 of them, found itself with a new nickname — "The Flying Brickyard"!

Over 70% of the Shuttle Orbiter's surface is protected by its special tiles. To keep costs down, the tiles were designed to be reusable for about 100 missions — the expected 'life span' of each Shuttle. Each tile carries a price tag of between $700 - $1,000 (about £350 - £500), so the total cost figure for tiling reads like a transatlantic telephone number!

The tiles are truly amazing. You can heat one until it is literally white-hot, and then pick it up with your bare fingers without feeling discomfort. Such heat containment allows for re-entry at temperatures of up to 700 degrees C (1,300 degrees F). The tiles vary in thickness from $\frac{1}{4}$ - $3\frac{1}{2}$ inches (6mm - 90mm), depending on the temperatures they must withstand.

These small squares of silica mean the difference between success and catastrophe on a Space Shuttle mission. If just one of them was to come adrift from a vital spot, then the craft and crew would be burned to a cinder in seconds. So when astronauts John Young and Bob Crippen lost radio contact as they began to re-enter the earth's atmosphere after the first Shuttle mission, the world held its breath and waited. As we now know, there was nothing to worry about — the tiles did their job to perfection and have continued to do so ever since.

The Shuttle is safe... thanks t its tiles

Fitting the tiles is a painstaking business. One mistake could easily lead to disaster. The black tiles are designed to withstand higher temperatures than the white ones.

ROTHERS & SISTERS

NICE OR NASTY
–TELL US
ABOUT THEM!

ICKS MY LOTHES!

y big brother is fashion-
d, and can't bear to be seen
ce in the same gear. His
swer to the problem is to
k MY clothes. I'm left shiv-
g while he's out enjoying
self, in MY jeans and
ater. And when he brings
clothes back, they're all
tched and torn, as he's
ger than me. He's driving
nuts!
n, Brighton.

SSING OUT SANTA

Christmas, when my brother Terry was small, my mum took
Christmas shopping in a big town. He was a bright kid, and
ced that there seemed to be an awful lot of Santas about, in the
ts and the department stores. Being puzzled, he asked Mum
t this, and she told him they were all simply Santa's helpers —
hief Santa Claus was, of course, in the North Pole where he
ld be. Mum thought Terry was quite satisfied with the
anation, and took him to see one of the toy department Santas.
went in to Santa's cave, and afterwards Mum could find no
of him whatever. A few minutes later, an annoyed-looking
a emerged from his dressing-room, pulling Terry by the hand.
ned out Santa had gone off duty after giving Terry his present,
e curious child had decided to follow him and see what was
on. Of course, he'd seen Santa's real clothes hanging up, and
ed the truth. Mum was very cross with him, of course, but we
d a laugh later.
f, Nottingham.

BIRTHDAY BRATS

When I was told I had to go to my younger sister's
birthday, I didn't mind too much. I reckoned I could
just sneak off after I'd eaten as many crisps and sausage
rolls as I wanted, and leave the girls to their musical
chairs or whatever. Little did I know! For some reason,
all twenty of the giggling little monsters made an
immediate B-line for me! They all barged into my room,
insisted on taking out all my model planes and boats,
and didn't leave until they'd smashed half of them.
Frankly, I don't think they were 10-year-old girls at all
— I'm convinced they were Attila The Hun's hordes in
disguise! And to cap it all, after tea Mum made me give
them all a conjuring show, as magic is my hobby. They
kept teasing me and pointing out how all my tricks were
done — and when one went wrong, they fell about
laughing. Finally, they all came up to examine the
conjuring gear, and they wrecked some of the little
boxes and things I use. It's the last time I EVER go to a
girls' birthday party!
Peter, Birmingham.

IN BROTHER'S SHADOW

My older brother is great — and that's just the trouble! I recently
started at the same school as him, and I've found everyone
compares us. Alan is tall for his age, very clever at lessons, and
good at football and athletics. Everyone at school expected me to
be the same, but I'm quite ordinary, and don't look like my brother
at all. People have made it pretty clear they're disappointed in me,
and some of them have been really nasty. I admire my brother, and
get on really well with him, but I can't help getting fed up. I keep
thinking that if we'd gone to different schools, people would have
just taken me as I am, and not expected so much of me. It's not fair!
Why on earth *should* everyone want me to be just like my big
brother?
Mark, London.

GOOD RIDDANCE TO THE SOUTH AMERICAN JUNGLE AND ITS CREATURES LIKE ANACONDAS AND PIRANHAS...

KANE BEGAN TO DREAM —

THE PIRANHAS — THE WAY THEY KILLED HIM — STRIPPED HIS FLESH! UGHH!

THEN —

OH, I'VE BEEN DOZING — HAVING A NIGHTMARE AND WE HAVEN'T EVEN TAKEN OFF YET...

THEN KANE SAW MEN APPROACHING ALONG THE AIRCRAFT —

OH, NO — SOUTH AMERICAN POLICE! SOMEHOW THEY MUST KNOW I MURDERED SIR JOHN! GOT TO MAKE A BREAK —

UH —?

GRAB MY GOLD AND GET OFF THE PLANE!

I DID IT! NOW TO GET OFF THE RUNWAY AND HIDE!

I'M IN THE JUNGLE. NOW I SLIP INTO A NEIGHBOURING SOUTH AMERICAN COUNTRY AND GET ANOTHER PLANE. HA — I'LL STILL GET OUT OF HERE!

Everlasting Magic o

A model of the spaceship in which Dan Dare made his death-defying journeys is among the treasured possessions of Dan Dare fan Alan Vince.

LIFE would have been deadly dull without the "Eagle" when I was a boy. Of all its wonderful contents, the stories I loved most of all were those about the most famous space adventurer of all time, Dan Dare.

The real secret behind Dan Dare's success, and for that matter "Eagle's", was the painstaking time spent on the drawings and scripts. Dan Dare led the way for a big revolution in British comics.

In "Eagle's" wake came many similar comics that gave new life to the comic strip industry and made household names of countless fictional characters and their artists. In planning the "Eagle", Marcus Morris, the Editor, called on the talents of a young artist named Frank Hampson. Frank, once he was let loose on Dan Dare, found he had a natural ability to write and illustrate a feature that was, in many ways, far ahead of its time.

The whole Dare creation was Frank's; he wrote the earlier stories until 1954, and was chief artist on the feature until 1959. In a way he was illustrating his dreams and ambitions for the future, creating a believable set of characters with all the right hardware. When it came to villains he also created the best — The Mekon.

Originally, the Hampson involvement in "Eagle's" early issues had not been solely Dan Dare. He had drawn the Tommy Walls colour strip, drawn and done research on the back-page story of St Paul and been involved for a time on the Rob Conway black and white strip.

Frank found it necessary to use a team for a number of reasons; first his workload for the earlier "Eagle"; second he was partly responsible for recruiting many of the artists who would later take over the regular strips when "Eagle" got settled and its future was assured. But mainly the team was there for Dan Dare's future, a future Frank hoped and dreamed would launch his creation into films, American comics and a whole new commercial enterprise. As Frank once put it, "I wanted the studio set-up to be the basis of something really big, in the way Walt Disney studios grew on the success of Mickey Mouse."

I suppose we could have even seen a Dan Dare Wonderland, where people could travel to Venus, Mars, Saturn, Cryptos and Terra Nova and see full-size models of Treens and Phants. Frank Hampson certainly had plans, but they, sadly, never became reality.

During his time with "Eagle", Frank Hampson was assisted by many artists on the Dan Dare strip. The list reads like a Who's Who of British cartoonists.

The original Dan Dare studio set-up was first class. At times, using the talents of three or four artists, Frank was producing some of the best strip cartoon work ever seen. The ground floor of his home was turned into three studios; the main one was Frank's, in which he had, apart from his drawing board, files, models and countless reference books and magazines. The models were of characters' heads, robots, space stations and spaceships.

There was the big red Crypt ship, the SFJ2 space station from the Red Moon story, the rescue ship from Operation Saturn (this large model actually opened up to display a detailed interior), and the Anastasia, Dan's personal little spacecraft presented to him by Sondar, his Treen friend, in appreciation for the original defeat of the Mekon.

Human Model

Frank would sometimes set up one of the models to draw from, thus ensuring a very accurate representation of each well-known craft.

As he once joked; "I had to be very careful in those days, if a spaceship, car or even a building wasn't quite right, we would get letters from Eagle-eyed readers saying so! That is why I tried very hard to keep the Dare strip believable, making the characters look and act like real people. I wanted them to look as if they had families back home, blood pressure, human weaknesses. Dan himself was never a superhero, he got plenty of knocks!"

By far the most moving touch in the strip was Frank's use of his own father, Robert Hampson, as the model for Space Fleet Controller, Sir Hubert Guest. This charac-

ter became so popular that some readers used to beg Frank not to kill him off, they began to love him as their own father. This, of course, meant a lot to Frank.

There also existed a large model of the space fleet headquarters. By plotting a route on this, Frank could always ensure that in certain frames the correct buildings or launching ramps would be in the backgrounds of his pictures.

People marvel at the visual effects of *Star Wars* and *Close Encounters of the Third Kind*. In "Eagle's" heyday, there weren't many classic science fiction films. So we relied on the visual impact of the strip cartoon and here Dan Dare was supreme.

Frank Hampson's natural talent for illustrating science fiction made the Dare stories not only exciting, but visually interesting. The stories themselves could last a year or more, building-up carefully the characters and plot.

I well recall the way in which the various races on Venus were introduced: first the Atlantines (descendants of Earth people taken to Venus by the Treens many centuries before) who were blue; then the Treens, cold, ruthless scientists ruled by the Mekon, they were green; lastly (living in the southern hemisphere) there were the brown Therons who, unlike the Treens, were peaceful and friendly towards the Earthmen.

Frank Hampson had managed with skilful drawing and scripting to mention much of the Treen/Atlantine/Theron history in the first story.

When the Red Moon threatened Earth,

"...TO FINISH THE GREEN FIEND!"

BY GEORGE, YES! — IT'S THAT TINY SATURNIAN.

we had vivid illustrations showing how the original inhabitants of Mars had perished from an attack by the same rogue asteroid. Similarly, when the evil Black Cats from Saturn first attacked Earth, Frank Hampson used drawings that enhanced the mystery and tension, making you eager to see next week's episode.

When Dan and his friends first approached Cryptos, they were attacked by Phant raiders and, again, Frank's most cinematic way of building the mystery and tension came to the fore.

We see Phant fighters zooming in on the Crypt ship as it closes on Cryptos; then a shot of the Phant Pilot, from behind, as he lines up his target; still not seeing his face, we get a close-up of one of the Phant's evil eyes looking into his gun-sights . . . it's really *Star Wars* material, years before this film was thought of.

At its peak "Eagle" used many top class artists, people who were experts in their field. Apart from Frank Hampson on Dan Dare, we had Frank Humphris drawing the western strip, Riders of the Range. This feature was written by BBC radio script writer, Charles Chilton. Both Frank and Charles were experts on the West. Most of the back page stories were illustrated by artists who were second to none in the field of historical costume and storytelling.

Being interested in "Eagle", I wanted to know more about the people behind the strips. One summer I went to Olympia to see the Hulton's Boys' and Girls' Exhibition. The whole main hall was decorated

with large Dan Dare spaceships. It was a great sight: Crypt ships one end, Treen fighters and space helicopters the other. There was a space station in the centre and large murals at each end of the hall, one depicting Earth and the moon, and the other one showing Saturn from one of its moons.

There was a special Dan Dare Studio set up on one of the stands.

These two illustrations of Dan Dare show perfectly the contrasting art styles of D.D., as drawn by Ian Kennedy (left) for the new EAGLE, with that of Frank Hampson's hero.

Working away at a drawing board surrounded by original artwork and models was Frank's assistant, Don Harley.

The detail and delicate colouring made me realise that the printed page just didn't do justice to the artwork. My mother managed to get me Don's autograph, and all too soon this highlight of my summer holiday was over.

In the 1950s, "Eagle" entertained with "Riders of the Range" and instructed with such features as this cutaway drawing of one of the Royal Family's cars.

JEFF ARNOLD IN *Riders of the Range*

A Royal Car

Readers of yesterday, who loved the exciting stories in the "Eagle" of the '50s and '60s, are succeeded by a new generation of youngsters who thrill to the exploits of Dan Dare and his friends in the new "Eagle".

While I continued to read "Eagle" during my art school years and when I started work, there had been a number of changes. In the 'Sixties, "Eagle" began to take on a different look. After illustrating the Life of Christ, Frank Hampson had left "Eagle", and I lost touch with him until the early 'Seventies. Keith Watson was the artist on Dan Dare for most of the Sixties, and he and I corresponded for a couple of years, lost touch and then met up again in 1977. I had made up my mind to track down as many of the old "Eagle" team as possible: I finally re-established contact with Frank Hampson in 1973 and in the following years met the other artists.

A handful of "Eagle" enthusiasts staged a convention in London in 1980 to celebrate the paper's 30th Birthday. Many of "Eagle's" staff were there, including Frank Hampson and Marcus Morris. We gave slide lectures, interviews, staged artwork displays and even had a special Dan Dare room which included a large Mekon sculpture.

The fact that I had kept all my back numbers of "Eagle", "Eagle" Annuals and the Dan Dare books led to a number of interesting requests in the late 'Seventies. In 1974, I had conducted a lengthy interview with Frank Hampson, which was later published in three parts in a fan mag called "Thing". This was shortly before Frank received an award from the Italian Comics Convention in Lucca in 1975.

He had gone to the gathering as a guest and was more than surprised to learn that he had been voted Best Post-War Strip Cartoonist, and received the Yellow Kid Award. The next year, 1976, I was asked by comics historian Denis Gifford to produce a Dan Dare slide lecture at his big "Comics 101" convention in London.

This convention was to mark the 100th anniversary of British comic art, and Frank Hampson was a guest along with other top-ranking British artists.

Following "101", Frank and I did talks at conventions in London, Brighton and

Early "Eagle" annuals and modern Dan Dare books are the prized possessions of Dan Dare's number one fan, Alan Vince.

Birmingham! Frank was also asked t[o] produce two large murals for the Londo[n] Science Museum's Space Exploration dis[]plays. Roger Dean, the designer and illus[]trator, was at that time associated with th[e] *Dragon's Dream* publishing company an[d] they had expressed interest in reprintin[g] some of the Dan Dare stories in bookform[.]

Using my copies of "Eagle" and som[e] new artwork by Frank and Don Harley[,] there have, to date, been three Dan Dar[e] books, *The Man From Nowhere, Rogu[e] Planet* and *Reign of the Robots*. Added t[o] this, Dragon's Dream also publishe[d] Frank's *Road of Courage* (the story o[f] Christ) in book form and a double Fran[k] Bellamy *High Command*, featuring his tw[o] strips for "Eagle", based on the lives of Si[r] Winston Churchill and Field Marsha[l] Montgomery. A fourth Dan Dare boo[k] *Safari in Space*, was to follow.

My keen interest in the work of Gerr[y] Anderson led me to fulfil another ambitio[n] in 1981. Allied to the popularity of Gerry'[s] TV puppet shows like *Stingray, Thunder[]birds* and *Captain Scarlet*, a new comic ha[d] been launched called "TV21". Many of th[e] artists who had worked on "Eagle" ha[d] moved to "TV21", among them Frank Hampson. As with "Eagle", Britain seeme[d] slow in fully appreciating its home-grow[n] talent and it wasn't until 1981 that the firs[t] Gerry Anderson convention was staged i[n] England.

At this I met a young modelmake[r] named Martin Bower, who had worked o[n] such TV shows as Gerry's *Space 1999*, and BBC's *Dr Who* and *Blake's 7*, and such feature films as *Alien, Flash Gordon* and *Outland*. Martin, it turned out, had made a number of models for the *Dan Dare* TV series and we agreed to see if he could make a few Dare models for me.

Frank Hampson has suffered a couple o[f] strokes that may well prevent him from drawing again. This talented artist and writer is also a man of great courage, having fought a battle against cancer. What does remain of his work on *Dan Dare* can only continue to inspire and influence those of us lucky enough to see it. Here's to Daniel Dare and his crew. May their adventures never end, and may the magic remain forever!

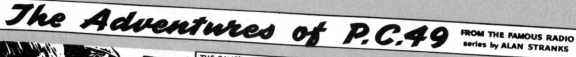

The Adventures of P.C.49

FROM THE FAMOUS RADIO series by ALAN STRANKS

A FAMOUS BRITISH EXPRES

*Reproduced from 'Eagle'
issue dated 24th November, 1950*

1. Rudder. 2. Starboard propellers. 3. After starboard engine room. 4. Control platform. 5. Forward starboard engine room. 6. Oil fuel tanks in double bottom. 7. After starboard boiler rooms. 8. Boiler uptakes to after-funnel. 9. Turbo-generator room. 10. Forward starboard boiler rooms. 11. Boiler uptake to fore-funnel. 12. Oil fuel tanks. 13. Tourist cabins. 14. Tourist dining room and galley. 15. First-class cabins. 16. Navigating bridge. 17. Motor-driven lifeboats (26 in all). 18. Air intake vents. 19. First-class hall and library. 20. Main staircase and lifts. 21. First-class swimming pool. 22. First-class restaurant. 23. Barber's shop and doctor's consulting room (under). 24. First-class lounge. 25. First-class saloon and ballroom. 26. First-class smoking room. 27. Main galley and pantries. 28. Cabin-class cabins. 29. Lift. 30. Cinema-theatre, seating 380. 31. Verandah grill-room. 32. Cabin-class smoking room. 33. Cabin lounge. 34. Staircase and lift. 35. Refrigerated stores. 36. Cabin-class swimming pool. 37. Baggage lift. 38. Crew's quarters. 39. Docking bridge.

E "GOLDEN ARROW"

The world-famous train seen leaving Victoria on its 95 minutes' dash to Dover Marine, where passengers embark on the Cross Channel steamer for Calais and thence by the French "Fleche d'or" to Paris. This 3-cylinder, 4-6-2 Merchant Navy Class Locomotive weighs 142½ tons.

1. Firebox and brick arch. 2. Siphon water circulators through firebox. 3. Driver's regulator and steam entry valve. 4. Steam pipe to superheater. 5. Superheater. 6. Superheater boiler flues. 7. Fire tubes for heating water. 8. Superheated steam pipes to cylinders. 9. Patent piston valves and rocker arm. 10. Piston on backward stroke. 11. Exhaust to middle cylinder exhaust and blast pipe. 12. Lemaitre multi-blast jets. 13. Steam pipe to middle cylinder. 14. Middle cylinder. 15. Bulleid valve motion to all three cylinders totally encased in an oil bath. 16. Crank of middle cylinder. 17. Crank of outside cylinder. 18. Cylinder drain cocks. 19. All-electric lighting-code discs above. 20. Wind deflectors. 21 Air intake lifting exhaust upwards away from driver's vision. 22. Safety valves. 23. Spun glass boiler insulation. 24. Pressed steel disc wheels. 25. Brake hangers. 26. Firebox draught dampers. 27. Tender water filler (5,000 gallons capacity). 28. Coal (five tons). 29. One of the nine first-class Pullmans.

RLD'S LARGEST LINER — THE "QUEEN ELIZABETH"

The "stateliest ship in being" was how "Eagle" described this 83,673-ton British luxury liner in December, 1950. She was 1,030 ft long and 118 ft in width. She carried a crew of 1,100 and had accommodation for 2,300 passengers. Her speed was 29 knots.

Reproduced from 'Eagle' issue dated 1st December, 1950

Harris Tweed, EXTRA SPECIAL AGENT

WHICH WAY WHIRLS THE WATER?

AWAY the water goes as you zip the plug out of the hole — giving science a problem that's been haunting it for years.

Does the water swirl away clockwise or anti-clockwise? And whichever way it goes, is it a fact that in the opposite hemisphere to the one your bathroom's in, the water runs away in the opposite direction?

This little mystery has been the subject of conjecture for ages, but only recently have scientists been giving it serious attention.

During the past few years, in laboratories as far apart as Australia, West Germany and Massachusetts, USA, investigators have been solemnly emptying the water from ordinary baths and specially-constructed water tanks and bowls in order to watch what happens.

When you pull out the plug, watch which way the bath water turns as it gurgles away. Scientists here and Down Under have been trying to work out why it swirls one way here and another way south of the equator.

The basic theory was simple. The Earth's own rotation, seen from the northern hemisphere, is anti-clockwise. Your bathwater gets pulled around by the momentum of the spinning globe and so also rotates anti-clockwise.

Down Under, in the southern hemisphere, from where the Earth's rotation is seen as a spinning movement in a clockwise direction, the water swirls away clockwise, too, according to the theory.

Investigators in Australia filled a large tank with water, let it settle for several hours and then pulled out the plug. "Clockwise rotation was observed," they duly reported.

The problem is by no means solved. The Australian researchers believe that one can never prove that small air currents don't dictate which way the water disappears. So the experiments go on.

Water experts in West Germany found that bath water develops a kind of memory. It seemed to remember which way it always swirled and always ran away in the same direction. Which is another puzzle to be solved!

THE ARMY THAT VANISHED

FOR obvious reasons more people disappear during war than at any other time. However, one of the strangest disappearances took place during World War One. In August, 1915, a whole battalion of Allied soldiers vanished during the Gallipoli campaign in the Dardanelles. The mystery deepened 50 years later when three witnesses made a startling official statement about the incident.

The Turks entered the war on Germany's side in October, 1914, and in April the following year a force of Commonwealth and French troops landed at the Gallipoli Peninsula. The idea was to seize the Dardanelles, a narrow strait joining the Aegean Sea with the Sea of Marmara, knock Turkey out of the war and open a supply route to Russia.

On 12th August, 1915, during an advance on Hill 60 in Sulva Bay, the First-Fifth Battalion of the Royal Norfolk Regiment disappeared. Later the decomposing bodies of less than half of the men were found, but the fate of the other troops is not known.

Eye-witnesses

On the 50th jubilee of the landings, however, F. Reichardt, R. Newnes and J.L. Newman, veterans of a New Zealand field company involved in the campaign, stated they had seen exactly what had happened to the Norfolks.

According to their statement, 12th August was a bright, clear day, except for the sky over Hill 60. From their vantage point overlooking the hill, the New Zealanders could see a strange formation of six or eight clouds hovering some 150 metres above the ground.

Each was identical and shaped like a loaf of bread. Below these, resting on the ground and straddling a dry creek bed, was a similar cloud about 245 metres in length, 60 metres wide and 65 metres high.

> **Three soldiers watched in disbelief as they saw their comrades disappear into the strange cloud formation which hovered over the battlefield called Hill 60**

All the clouds were light grey and, although there was a heavy breeze, they remained motionless.

As though in a trance, several hundred men of the First-Fifth Norfolks marched up the hill and into the large cloud without hesitation.

After about an hour, when the last trooper had entered it, the cloud lifted, joined those waiting above and drifted slowly off to the north. Hill 60 was deserted, nobody could be seen in the area.

Never Found!

The Regiment was posted missing or captured, but after the war the British demanded the Turks return whatever remained of the men. Turkey replied she had made no contact with the Regiment or had any knowledge that it existed. *The missing men were never found*!

The New Zealanders' statement came in for much criticism, especially as the Allies had attacked Hill 60 nine days later (on 21st August, 1915) during heavy mist and were almost wiped out in the battle.

Had Reichardt and his comrades got the dates confused and simply imagined they saw the men vanish during a fierce battle? Were they so afraid of ridicule they waited until 1965 before telling their strange story?

Disaster

The Dardanelles was a disaster for the Allies; they lost over 34,000 troops before they abandoned the enterprise in November, 1915.

In all 27,000 of these men have no known grave and one wonders how many of these casualties met the same fate as the lost battalion of Hill 60!

Conditions in the Dardanelles were appalling in that hot summer of 1915. Many wounded men died from fever and infection. Fifty years later, fragments of the fallen and their equipment from the Gallipoli landings were still being washed up onto the beaches by the Aegean Sea, to remind everyone of this terrible campaign.

HOW GOOD A JOE SOAP ARE YOU?

Continued

watch the reaction you get.

B) Pretend you found the bag lying in the street and accidentally discovered the cash.

C) Keep the cash and refuse to return it until you get a satisfactory explanation.

8. Finally, all is revealed at the restaurant and it turns out that the Chinese always eat Indian take away food and vice-versa. The cash was simply for payment and the 'Chef special' idea was a clever way of making sure that the money was never stolen. (I mean, who goes round nicking trays of rice?) How would you end this disaster?

A) Hurl an omelette at the new Chinese waiter.

B) Resolve to close the office an hour earlier next Friday.

C) Ask if there's any more Chef's special to pay for your trouble.

SCORING

1. A, 0 points. B, 2 points. C, 5 points. This way you're sure to get something out of the case.

2. A, 0. B, 5. C, 5. This way the food can be collected and you can be around to discover the identity of the collector.

3. A, 0. B, 2. C, 5. This way you're not revealing that you know anything, and it's less messy than knocking all the food over!

4. A, 5. B, 2. C, 0. The simplest, most direct way.

5. A, 2. B, 0. C, 5. If in doubt — get out!

6. A, 5. B, 0. C, 2. Ask the chap, after all he's your 'Client'.

7. A, 0. B, 5. C, 2. Your story is just about believable, and the manager must give you some sort of explanation.

8. A, 0. B, 5. C, 2. Close early and save yourself all the hassle.

RATING

40-28. You're thinking on the lines that I do. (Is that praise?) Well done, fellow Soaper!

27-16. Some shrewd moves. Maybe you could be my assistant. Unpaid, of course!

15-0. Sorry. Stick to watching the Rockford Files!

Ernie's LAUGH

NEXT TIME YOU COME WITH ME WHEN I'M SWIMMING THE CHANNEL — DON'T FORGET YOUR OARS!

GOOD MORNING, — I REPRESENT THE ER, AH, UM, THE ER.....

MEMORY COURSE

EAGL ONE-LINER

What's red a lies in the middle of the road?
A dead bus!

What's green and turns red the flick of a switch?
Kermit in a liquidiser!

What did Nelson say to his men before they got on the ship?
Men, get on the ship!

SGT. STREETWISE

FOR GEORGE TAGGART OF THE METROPOLITAN POLICE SPECIAL UNDERCOVER DIVISION A WORKING DAY STARTED WITH A TRIP THROUGH A SUBWAY...

HOLD ON, WILLY— HERE COMES A LIKELY PUNTER!

HERE, WATCH WHERE YOU'RE GOING, GRANDPA!

OOOOFF!

I SAW THAT. KIDS HAVE GOT NO MANNERS THESE DAYS. I BLAME THE PARENTS.

THE LITTLE PERISHER KNOCKED THE WIND OUT OF ME!

HEY— MY WALLET'S GONE! HE MUST HAVE STOLEN IT!

WHERE'S MY WALLET?

I'M CLEAN, GUV', HONEST. SEARCH ME IF YOU WANT.

THAT'S BECAUSE BATES SWITCHED THE WALLET TO ME WHEN WILLY SYKES DISTRACTED THE MUG.

SATISFIED? NOW HOP IT BEFORE I CALL THE LAW.

CLEAN AS A WHISTLE.

TAGGART IMMEDIATELY CONTACTED 'S TOP UNDERCOVER OPERATOR, DETECTIVE-SERGEANT WISE...

MORNIN', **UNCLE GEORGE** WHAT'S THE GRIM FACE FOR?

SOMEBODY'S JUST STOLEN MY WALLET.

AND...

SOUNDS LIKE THE BIG BLOKE WAS A DECOY WHILE THE KID SWITCHED THE WALLET TO ANOTHER MATE.

THAT'S HOW I FIGURED IT. I'VE BEEN THROUGH OUR MUG SHOTS. LOOK...

THE KID IS 'CHUMMY' BATES, STRICTLY A SMALL TIME THIEF. THE UGLY ONE IS WILLY SYKES, HE'S GOT 'A' LEVELS IN GBH.

IT'S YOUR CASE NOW, WISE. I WANT YOU TO BREAK THIS LITTLE PICK-POCKETING OPERATION FOR GOOD!

MEANWHILE, SYKES AND BATES WERE STILL AT 'WORK'—

I'M GOING TO KNOCK YOUR BLOCK OFF, SONNY JIM.

I DIDN'T TAKE YOUR FLAMIN' WALLET... HONEST.

S'CUSE ME, SIR.

IF THERE'S ANY BLOCKS TO BE KNOCKED OFF...I'LL DO IT!

UGHHH!

PHEW — HE TURNED REAL NASTY!

FORGET HIM. LET'S GET OVER TO 'FAGUNS' AND DIVVY UP THE TAKINGS.

AT FAGUN THE FENCE'S SHOP...

A POLICE ID CARD. YOU IDIOT, BATES. ONE OF THE PUNTERS WAS 'OLD BILL'!

HOW WAS I TO KNOW?

MY DEAR WILLY — CALM DOWN, WILL YOU?

THERE'S THIRTY QUID IN THE WALLET. I'M NOT FUSSY IF IT'S FUZZ MONEY.

IT'S ALL RIGHT FOR YOU, FAGUN — ME AND MY 'DIPS' TAKE ALL THE RISKS.

IF YOU DON'T LIKE IT, DEAR BOY... GO ELSEWHERE. BUT I KNOW I PAY YOU THE BEST PRICES IN TOWN FOR YOUR ILL-GOTTEN GAINS.

LET'S GET IT STRAIGHT. I DON'T LIKE YOU AND I DON'T TRUST YOU. SO KEEP PAYING ME TOP PRICES OR I'M LIKELY TO GET VERY UPSET.

THE NEXT EVENING...

SYKES' SET-UP SOUNDS IF IT'S ORGANISED. I'LL TRY AND DEAL MYSELF IN ON IT.

THERE THEY ARE. I'LL INTRO-DUCE MYSELF BY ATTEMPTING A CLUMSY 'DIP'—

HERE — WATCH IT!

SORRY!

NO YOU DON'T, LITTLE MAN!

WHAT'S UP?

GOOD... HE FELT ME LIFT HIS WALLET.

'DIP' ME, WOULD YOU?

I DIDN'T MEAN IT, GUV! I'M DOWN AND OUT... LIVING ROUGH.

AND I LIKE MY FACE THE WAY IT IS, MATE.

OOFFAAA!

I-I OUGHT TO TEAR YOU TO BITS. BUT MAYBE I CAN USE A SMART LAD. WHAT'S YOUR NAME?

ER—OLIVER!

79

OLLIE, THIS HERE'S CHUMMY BATES. HE'LL INTRODUCE YOU TO THE REST OF THE TEAM—

BATES IS JUST A KID.

AND—

MEET ARTY AND PETE. ON BUSY DAYS WE SOMETIMES WORK A FOUR-MAN OPERATION.

I HOPE YOU'RE AS GOOD AS CHUMMY. HE'S LEARNT THE TRADE REAL WELL.

DEPENDING ON HOW YOU WORK OUT— SYKES'LL TAKE YOU TO MEET FAGUN WHEN THE TIME'S RIGHT. HE FENCES THE CREDIT CARDS, WATCHES AND THAT. DRIVES A ROLLER AS WELL.

THAT'S THE GUY I'M AFTER.

SOON, WISE WAS DELIVERING TO SYKES...

SIX WALLETS AND ALL BULGING... I LIKE IT . . .

GOOD JOB I CAN GET A LOT OF WALLETS FROM POLICE STORES.

... LIKE IT VERY MUCH!

AND—

SO, IF WE BAG FAGUN WE NAIL THE WHOLE ORGANISATION, 'UNCLE' GEORGE.

SYKES? FAGUN? AND YOUR ALIAS IS OLIVER...

CHARLES DICKENS WOULD TURN IN HIS GRAVE.

MEET ME AT WORK TOMORROW AND I'LL LET YOU HAVE WHAT NEWS I CAN...

AND, NEXT DAY...

I'LL TAKE THIS ONE, CHUMMY.

SURE THING.

SORRY, CHUM.

WHAT THE..?

JUST A NOTE TO TELL HIM THERE'S NO NEWS YET OF FAGUN'S ADDRESS.

NICE GOIN'.

IT WAS A DODDLE!

BUT I'M RUNNING OUT OF SPARE WALLETS FAST.

LATER—

OKAY, OLLIE— YOU'VE DONE SO WELL, IT'S TIME YOU MET WITH FAGUN.

GOOD. TAKE ME TO YOUR LEADER AND I CAN FINISH WITH THIS CASE.

BUT—

'ELLO, MR. WISE. DON'T FORGET THE RENT TOMORROW, YOU OWE TWO WEEKS.

MRS. PRATT, MY LANDLADY. THAT'S TORN IT.

I THOUGHT YOU WERE DOWN AND OUT, LAD?

STEAK AND KIDNEY FOR SUPPER TONIGHT, YOUR FAVOURITE.

IT'S TIME WE HAD A CHAT *MISTER WISE.*

AND, NEXT MORNING, WHEN BATES CALLED AT FAGUN'S TO FIND OUT WHAT HAD HAPPENED TO HIS PICK-POCKETING PARTNER . . .

OKAY, THAT LOOKS LIKE THE PLACE..LET HIM GO INSIDE FOR A MINUTE AND THEN WE MOVE IN — FAST !

INSIDE—

EASY, SYKES. YOU KNOW I LOATHE VIOLENCE, DEAR BOY.

I'LL MAKE HIM TALK. HE'S UNDER-COVER FUZZ, I KNOW HE IS.

THEN—

SYKES... FAGUN...THIS IS THE POLICE ! *YOU'RE BUSTED !*

CRIKEY—IT'S THE LAW !

OUT OF MY WAY, BRATS!

UGHHH!

THERE'S NO PLACE TO RUN TO, SYKES!

NO— DON'T BE A FOOL!

STAY BACK, COPPER, OR I'LL ...AAAAHH—

AIEEEEEE!

MEANWHILE—

OKAY, MR. FAGUN— I HOPE YOU'VE GOT A RECEIPT FOR EVERY ARTICLE IN THE PLACE.

MY LIFE, OFFICER, MY GREAT AUNT LEFT IT ALL TO ME IN HER WILL.

LATER—

YOU DID A GOOD JOB NABBING THE FAGUN MOB, WISE. BUT I DID MY BIT BY KEEPING A TAIL ON CHUMMY WHEN YOU WENT MISSING WITH SYKES.

I KNOW, UNCLE GEORGE. NOW CAN I HAVE *MORE*, PLEASE?

THE END.

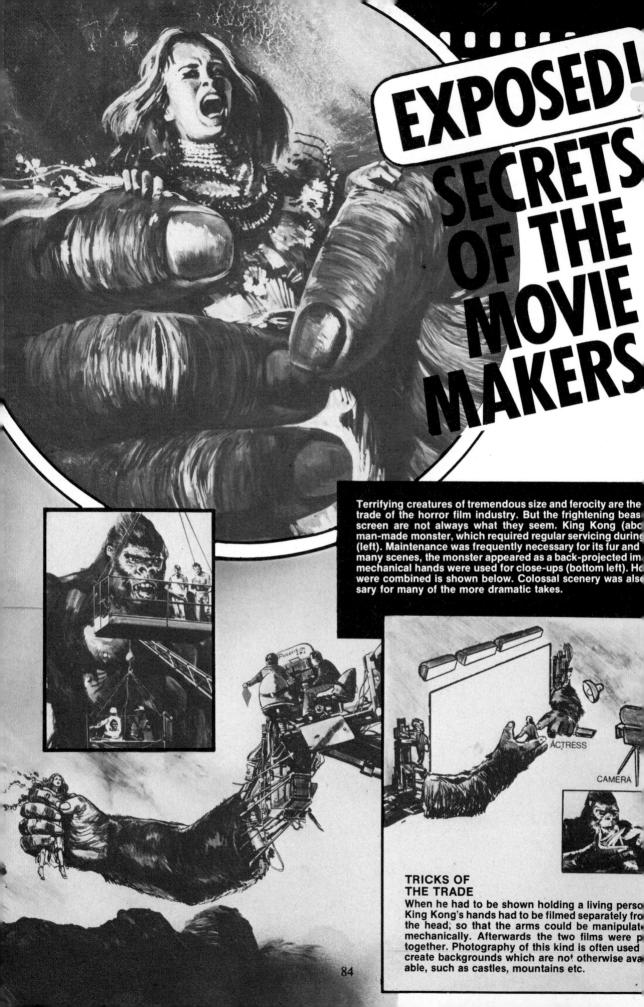

EXPOSED!
SECRETS OF THE MOVIE MAKERS

Terrifying creatures of tremendous size and ferocity are the
trade of the horror film industry. But the frightening beas
screen are not always what they seem. King Kong (abc
man-made monster, which required regular servicing durin
(left). Maintenance was frequently necessary for its fur and
many scenes, the monster appeared as a back-projected im
mechanical hands were used for close-ups (bottom left). Ho
were combined is shown below. Colossal scenery was als
sary for many of the more dramatic takes.

ACTRESS

CAMERA

TRICKS OF THE TRADE

When he had to be shown holding a living perso
King Kong's hands had to be filmed separately fro
the head, so that the arms could be manipulate
mechanically. Afterwards the two films were p
together. Photography of this kind is often used
create backgrounds which are not otherwise ava
able, such as castles, mountains etc.

creaming pitifully, the girl
struggled and kicked as the tow-
ering ape picked her up from the
[t]h the jungle clearing and held
[i]n high.

ave me!" she shrieked. "Save

e monster bared its teeth in a
and . . .

ut!" yelled the director, thrusting
cigar into his mouth. "Let's run
that scene again."

the vast movie set on which this
was being shot, technicians
[ed] the equipment that con-
[e]d the enormous ape. This great
al, built upon an aluminium
[le]ton with cables and hydraulic
instead of veins and arteries, was
[ex]ample of the hard work which
[went] into creating the illusions you see
[on] the screen.

[M]en are made to appear weightless,
[h]istoric monsters become alive,
[wor]lds collide in space and warriors
[en]ge in sword fights with mytholog-
[ical] creatures.

[H]ow these illusions are created is
[fasci]nating. The giant ape was made
[for t]he film "King Kong". For some of
[the s]cenes the ape, or such parts of him
[w]ere required, such as his hands,
[were] photographed against a blue
[scre]en in the studio.

[A] film was produced in which the
[blue] backing was shown as clear film,
[with] the foreground action retained. A
[print]er then combined the foreground
[el]ement with a background scene,
[such] as a jungle. When the two films
[were] combined, it appeared that the
[acto]rs were really in a jungle.

[In] this way, King Kong's mechani-
[cal h]ands could be filmed in the foreground and afterwards combined with
shots of his head in the background, so
that he really appeared to be holding
something and looking at it.

Horrifying effects were produced
for the film "Jaws". The part was
played by a real shark in some scenes
and by three different mechanical
sharks in others. One could only be
filmed from the right, because its
machinery was exposed on the left.
Another had its working parts
exposed on the right, and was filmed
from the left.

A third model was a complete shark
that was towed behind a boat and used
for overhead shots. The others were
packed with hydraulic, pneumatic and
electronic equipment.

Each was attached by a boom to a
sunken platform. Worked by remote
control, the boom — or arm — gave
the shark movement, raising it to the
surface as well as causing it to leap out
of the water and dive back into it.

Sea Beast

Monsters of many frightening kinds
have been created for films. Among
them was a horrifying sea animal
which was seen in "The Creature
From The Black Lagoon". This was
part-fish and part-reptile and the size
of a man. Its costume was worn by a
skilled swimmer, who was able to stay
under water for five minutes before
surfacing for air.

The people who make the models
move are called animators. Their
work consists of making a model. This
is photographed one picture — or
frame — at a time and moved a
fraction for each frame. When the
animated model and the live actors are

Hatred glared from the eyes of the deadly
shark in "Jaws", which was made in three
mechanical versions, two with the machinery exposed on alternate sides.

REAR PROJECTOR   SCREEN

ACTOR

CAMERA

In "The Incredible Shrinking Man", the illusion of a
miniature human was made by combining film of a man,
photographically reduced, with that of a door and cat.

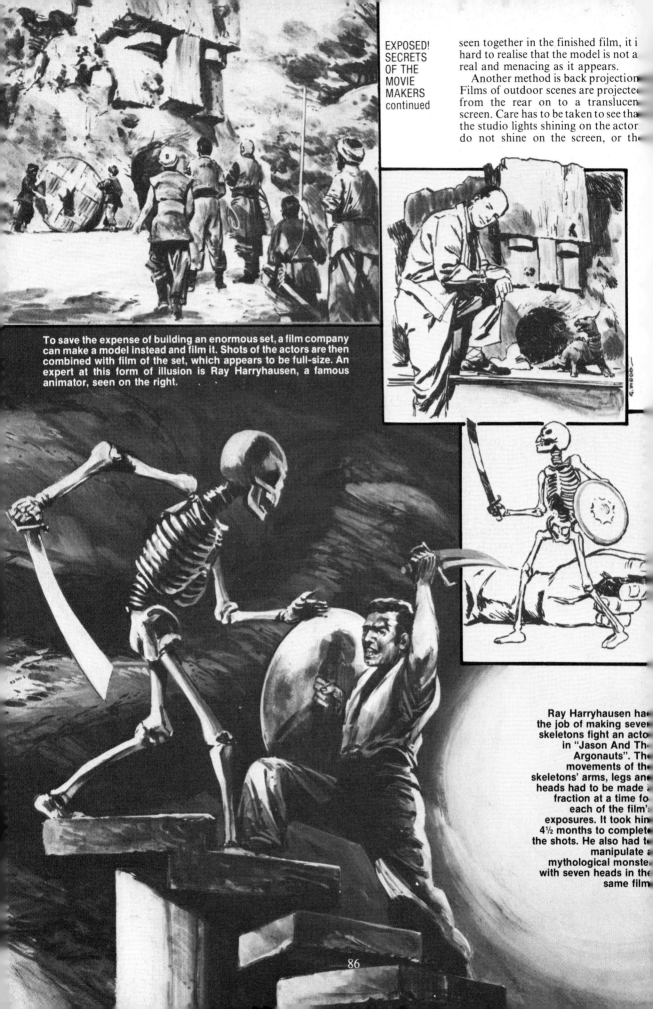

EXPOSED!
SECRETS
OF THE
MOVIE
MAKERS
continued

seen together in the finished film, it i
hard to realise that the model is not a
real and menacing as it appears.

Another method is back projection
Films of outdoor scenes are projecte
from the rear on to a translucen
screen. Care has to be taken to see tha
the studio lights shining on the actor
do not shine on the screen, or th

To save the expense of building an enormous set, a film company can make a model instead and film it. Shots of the actors are then combined with film of the set, which appears to be full-size. An expert at this form of illusion is Ray Harryhausen, a famous animator, seen on the right.

Ray Harryhausen ha
the job of making seve
skeletons fight an acto
in "Jason And Th
Argonauts". The
movements of th
skeletons' arms, legs an
heads had to be made
fraction at a time fo
each of the film'
exposures. It took hi
4½ months to complet
the shots. He also had t
manipulate
mythological monste
with seven heads in th
same film

The soldier is a stunt man in a flameproof suit, with an unseen oxygen mask and cylinders sewn into his clothing. The shots fired by the gangster above are blanks, the explosions being made by squibs embedded in the desk. Wall-walking (below) is possible if the wall is really the floor and the set and camera are turned on their sides. The desk, chair and the man's shoes are fixed with screws.

projected picture would be fainter at that spot.

Front projection is also used. The background is projected on to a screen made of glass particles, which reflect light back to its source. As the picture is projected through a two-way mirror at 45 degrees to the projector, the picture is returned to the mirror through which it passes to a camera.

Actors appearing before the screen mask any shadows they create, and light shining on them does not spoil the background, because the screen returns this light to its source.

Wall-Walking

A famous animator, Ray Harry-hausen, brought seven skeletons to life for "Jason And The Argonauts". It took him 4½ months to film the animation. He had to manipulate the arms, legs and heads of seven skeletons and combine them with the movements of three people, hacking away at each other with swords.

"The Seventh Voyage of Sinbad" called for the actors to enter a cave, which was the mouth of a giant stone face carved in a rock. A miniature of the stone face was made months after the live action had been shot. The shots of the two — the model and the actors — were combined so well that the trick was undetectable.

Walking up a wall is another thing actors can seem to do. This is done by building the film set on its side, so that the man on the wall is really standing on the floor. The man at the desk is the

A brawl in the Wild West and two crooks get their deserts. Both events seem lethal, but they are safe because the victims are stunt men and the "glass" is a harmless, brittle resin that breaks without causing an injury. The window frame is of balsa wood.

one fighting gravity in our picture. The table, chair and even his shoes are screwed to the wall. By putting the camera on its side, the illusion of a wall-walker is created.

If the sight of an eerie, misty church-yard with figures flitting about in the gloom makes you worried, calm down. The mist is blown out by a machine and is a mixture of frozen carbon dioxide and vaporised oil.

A fight which ends with the loser being thrown through a glass window is not as dangerous as it looks if the "glass" is resin. Being brittle, this shatters on impact and does not hurt the man, who lands on an unseen mattress.

Resin is also used for the bottles which are smashed realistically on people's heads, so nobody comes to harm. But a person could be in trouble

if a shot involving fire goes wro[ng]

For such scenes, stunt men a[re] employed. They wear flame-pr[oof] suits under their outer clothing, a[nd] an oxygen mask as well.

Sound effects add realism wh[en] shots are fired in a film. But to ma[ke] the result more authentic, you have [to] see what happens when the bul[let] strikes its target. Explosive squi[bs] which fling debris all over the pla[ce] are used for this.

Movie makers are now using co[m]puters and video recorders to mak[e a] 3-D image of, for example, a man. T[he] image moves eerily on the screen a[nd] gives viewers the impression that th[ey] are seeing right inside his head from [all] possible angles. The head also appe[ars] to turn, shrink and fade away — a ve[ry] eerie sensation!

But this is only a hint of some of t[he] incredible things that we will see [on] cinema and TV screens in the futu[re.]

Movie makers will be using scie[n]tific tools to develop an entirely n[ew] way of putting across a story — building dream fantasies we will [all] enjoy!

THE EN[D]

COMBAT TESTED!

In the fight for the Falklands, they ruled on land, sea and air!

SEA HARRIER JUMP JET

Up like a lift and forward like a jet. . . that's the Sea Harrier. Its secret is its four jet thrust nozzles, which swivel downwards for vertical take-off and backwards for forward propulsion and make it the only seagoing V/STOL aircraft in the West. Its rate of climb is 50,000 feet a minute, and its speed ranges from hover to 740mph at low level and over Mach 1 in a dive.

ROYAL NAVY

250

...dy by the mid-80s
...be the Sea Eagle, the
...skimming, anti-ship missile,
... fixed below the wing.
...pons are carried for anti-submarine,
...ce attack and air combat. Other
...ures are a raised cockpit and Blue Fox
... Harriers are built in the UK and USA.

...ki-ramp fitted to the bows of
... carrier aids the Sea Harrier's
...e-off, when the plane is
...ying a heavy load.

Sidewinder Missile

Wing fuel tanks

Fuselage fuel tanks

Rear fuel tanks

Radar warning receiver aerials

38 ROYAL NAVY

Pitch & yaw nozzle

Fox radar

Electronic & equipment packs

Pitch reaction nozzle

Rolls-Royce Pegasus Mk. 104 engine

30mm. Aden guns in external pods

Swivelling jet nozzles

Jettisonable 100 gal. combat tank

Roll-reaction nozzle

Retracted outrigger wheels

89

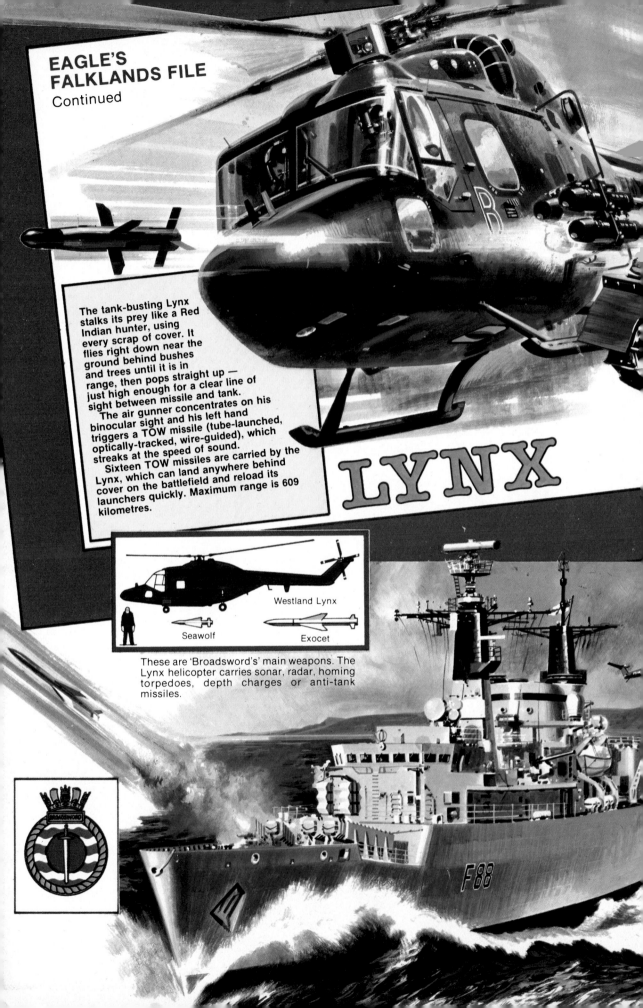

EAGLE'S FALKLANDS FILE
Continued

The tank-busting Lynx stalks its prey like a Red Indian hunter, using every scrap of cover. It flies right down near the ground behind bushes and trees until it is in range, then pops straight up — just high enough for a clear line of sight between missile and tank.

The air gunner concentrates on his binocular sight and his left hand triggers a TOW missile (tube-launched, optically-tracked, wire-guided), which streaks at the speed of sound.

Sixteen TOW missiles are carried by the Lynx, which can land anywhere behind cover on the battlefield and reload its launchers quickly. Maximum range is 609 kilometres.

LYNX

Westland Lynx

Seawolf

Exocet

These are 'Broadsword's' main weapons. The Lynx helicopter carries sonar, radar, homing torpedoes, depth charges or anti-tank missiles.

F88

02 FD 25

SCORPION

A tracked, reconnaissance combat vehicle. . . that's the Scorpion. It is lightly armoured to protect the crew against small arms fire, flying splinters and shrapnel. The Scorpion is one of a family of combat vehicles. Other versions are fitted with anti-tank missiles, anti-tank guns or quick-firing 30mm Rarden cannons. Scorpions also come as armoured personnel carriers, command vehicles or recovery vehicles — and they can all be made amphibious. With a top speed of 87km/h on good ground, its main task in battle is to explore the ground ahead of the main military body, so that the crew can bring back useful information.

'BROADSWORD' AND 'BRILLIANT' GO TO WAR

Among the Royal Navy's fleet in the Falklands were two Type 22 warships, 'Brilliant' and 'Broadsword'. With their four Rolls-Royce jet engines and their missiles, helicopters and computers, they packed plenty of punch. Two of the engines are Olympus types, similar to Concorde's. At full power, the four engines thrust the frigates through the water at 31 knots (33.75mph or 54.3km/h.). Deadly offensive and defensive fire power are carried. This includes Exocet missiles, which are long-range ship destroyers, more powerful and accurate than a whole battery of big guns.

Close range defence is provided by two 40mm cannon. Also on board is the Seawolf, a short range defender, and a Lynx helicopter.

The frigates' electronics, radar and communications equipment give the captain a detailed up-to-the-second picture of what is going on over a vast area around his ship and forewarn him of any potential threat.

Features include twin rudders and propellers, torpedo tubes, satellite communications and a gearbox which alters the engines' turning speed to the required propeller turning speed. The Lynx's hangar and landing deck are in the stern, and in the bows are the Exocet missiles in their launch containers.

SCIMITAR. Shorter range than Scorpion. Armed with a 30mm Rarden cannon. Support to main tank squadrons.

Wheeled variant of Scimitar, FOX is much quieter than its tracked counterparts and can travel on any terrain.

THE INCREDIBL

FOR the crew of the Lancaster bomber in the dark days of 1944, it was to have been a routine bombing raid on an industrial target. That is, if it could be called routine to defy anti-aircraft fire and the German air force's fast-firing fighters over enemy-occupied Europe.

As they taxied for the take-off on 21st June, at the height of the Second World War, the crew knew that they could expect trouble.

But they did not know that this trip was to be their toughest and deadliest.

Their target was a bomb-manufacturing plant at Wesseling in the Ruhr Valley, where many of Germany's war plants were sited.

As they were flying over the Dutch coast, Flying Officer Rackley, the plane's skipper, and his crew hit trouble.

A terrific explosion aft threw them into a steep dive. A shell from an anti-aircraft gun had scored a hit. Rackley and his flight engineer pulled at the control column with all their weight and managed to get the plane on a level keel.

Then they found that the plane they were flying was crippled. Damage to the control surfaces gave the plane a permanent veer to starboard. This could only be corrected by lashing the control column in the neutral position. It was also necessary to pass a rope around the starboard pedal and tie this to the framework.

A large hole had been burst open in the floor, forward of the rear turret.

Rackley set course for home. When they were over the English Channel, Taffy Davis, the rear-gunner, unclipped his parachute from the side of the fuselage and saw that it had been too damaged by gunfire to be of any use.

Entangled!

His only hope was to bale out, lashed to the bomb aimer. This is what he did, followed closely by other members of the crew.

The coast of England was by now in sight, but the Lancaster was losing power. The pilot had planned to fly his plane across England to the west coast and ditch it there.

But this plan had to be changed, for the aircraft was already doomed and had to be abandoned. Through the front escape hatch went the engineer, followed by the pilot, Rackley.

As he fell, Rackley heard his own plane spiralling in starboard turn earthwards. Suddenly, the sound o the engines stopped as an orange glov lit up the clouds below, succeeded by a shattering explosion.

Rackley floated down with hi parachute to the clouds. Once he wa among them, he found himself bein dragged along at a fast speed. Then h became aware of the sound of trair wheels rattling close to his head.

Although he did not realise it at th time, Rackley's parachute had becom entangled with a train.

What happened next was a blank ir Rackley's mind. He regainec consciousness to find himself beside railway line. It was dark and hi parachute had gone, dragged away by the train.

Feeling dazed, Rackley begar staggering along the line. His head wa: bleeding. All feeling had gone from hi: shoulders and his right arm hung limp and useless at his side.

He was near to complete collapse when another train approached Seeing the injured man, the drive stopped his train and took Rackley tc the nearest town, where he wa: hurried by ambulance to hospital.

All of the rest of the crew made safe

A terrific explosion aft threw the plane into a steep dive. Desperately, the pilot and his flight engineer pulled at the control column to right the plane. Would they succeed?

ESCAPE

descents, except Taffy Davis, the man without a parachute. He was descending, clinging to another parachutist, when he slipped from the man's grasp to his death.

He was the only fatality in a bad luck mission!

With his Lancaster bomber crippled by gunfire, the pilot floated earthwards on his parachute . . . straight into the path of a speeding train.

FAST FINISH

Higher and higher and faster and fas...
... records are tumbling every day. I
how much do you know about the worl
record breakers? Test your knowled
with the easy quiz belo

1. Three spacemen travelled at 24,791mph. Did
   occur in 1969, 1979 or 19
2. Gary Gabelich's record of 622.28mph was achie
   in the rocket-powered *Blue Flame*. Did he reach
   speed on water, in the air or on the la
3. Which racing driver has won 24 Grand Prix ra
   and become world champion five times? A J F
   Jackie Stewart or Juan-Manuel Fan
4. The Pronghorn antelope is the fastest of all
   animals. True or fa
5. Britain's fastest land animal is the Roe deer. W
   speed has one been known to rea
6. A French train reached 236mph on 26th Febru
   1981. Was this train called *Mistral*, *Tres Grand Vite*
   or *Faire un Sa*
7. What fuel was used to power the fastest fixed w
   aircraft in 1964? Was it kerosene, liquid oxygen
   ammonia, or high-octane gaso
8. How long did John Alcock
   Arthur Whitten-Brown take to fly
   Atlantic in 1919? Was their time 18 h
   36 hours or 16½ ho
9. *Sea Fury* achieved a record brea
   speed in 1966. Is this vehicle a ship
   aeroplane or a racing
10. During his racing career, Sir Go
    Richards won 4,870 races. Was h
    airman, jockey or run